Legends From The Forest

Legends From The Forest

TOLD BY CHIEF THOMAS FIDDLER

Edited by James R. Stevens

Translations by Edtrip Fiddler

PENUMBRA PRESS, 1985

Published by Penumbra Press, P.O.Box 340, Moonbeam,
Ontario, Canada POL 1VO, with assistance from The Canada
Council and The Ontario Arts Council.

Cover art is entitled *Yorkboat* by Levius Fiddler.

ISBN 0 920806 64 3

This book is dedicated to the memory of my father,
Chief Robert Fiddler, 1860-1940.

CONTENTS

Legends of Weesakayjac

Creatures

Duels with Neighbouring Clans

Legends of the Yorkboat Men

Heroes from the Past: Old Young Lad

Man Always Sitting

The Marten: James Linklater

Bears, Wolves

The Artists

Introduction

James R. Stevens

CANADA, one of the western nations, is most often thought of as an industrialized country in step with progressive technological advance. This is true of a narrow geographical sector of Canada that dominates its culture, economics and politics. This segment of the country above the American border is densely populated by people of mostly European extraction. Yet Canada is a giant of a country, the second largest on the globe, and a large portion of the land is dominated by the great boreal forest that covers the granitic shield area that crosses most of Canada from east to west. It is in the boreal forest that modern Canada quickly changes into a third world country where scattered native villages are common. This is especially true across northern Ontario, where some thirty villages are inhabited by native people whose roots date back into the pale. In Ontario, these people call themselves the Nishinawbe Aski Nation.

These people of the forest have a world view based on centuries of forest survival uninterrupted, until recently, by sedentary living, technology and Judeo Christian concepts of life. As a result of these changes, boreal culture in northern Ontario and northern Canada has not remained static in the twentieth century. Modern ways have been adopted into lifestyles. Snow machines have replaced dog teams. Radio and television are accessible media. A few young people have graduated from high schools, colleges and universities. Many variations of Christian doctrines are preached in boreal villages. Most of these incursions are less than three decades from inception and they have not completely obliterated all of the forest customs that have been passed along by elders.

The premier story teller of this book, Thomas Fiddler, is one of the many elders who has seen all the above changes come to his people. He remains strong in his tradition. Fiddler is the hereditary leader of the Sucker clan at Big Sandy Lake on the Upper Severn River in the province of Ontario. His father, Robert Fiddler, and grandfather, Jack Fiddler, were leaders before him. This lineage is traceable to a great grandfather who had no English name. He was the Porcupine Standing Sideways who died in 1891 at the ripe old age of 121 years.

But the selection of legends that Thomas Fiddler tells us are often older than the nineteenth century. Legends of Weesakayjac, the spirit being of humanity, reach back to early stone-age times. Thus, these legends are pre-Christian in origin and within this old native culture the language has no profanities. It is impossible to swear in the native tongue. References to sexual behaviour are told for humour. Often these sexual references are laughable because of the impossibility of certain acts. 'Weesakayjac Gives Birth' is an example of this type of legend. Other legends are told not for humour but for their lessons on life.

Other story tellers in this volume are friends of Thomas Fiddler. Both Edward Rae of clan Sturgeon and Titus Goodman of clan Sucker have passed away, while Thomas Linklater and Abel Fiddler are middle-aged men at Sandy Lake. Some legends these story tellers relate come from earlier days when young men fasted on the hills to seek dreams of creatures of the sky, land and water. Sometimes visionary dreams presented to the dreamer a protector who could be called on when needed. The legend *Crow Visits the North Wind* deals with a boreal man who sends a crow off to see his spiritual protector, the North Wind. Some dreams gave individuals the necessary powers to operate the shaking tent. This mystical medium was used to communicate with creatures and people in the spirit world. It was used to cure, as in the story *Marten Cures Thomas Fiddler* and often this strange tent was used to prophesy events. Much of this 'magic' gained in fasting is viewed as sacrilegious by people with Christian rearing, but as Thomas Fiddler said when he began telling these legends: 'What I am going to tell you has been told among my people for generations and there is no reason anyone should look down at these stories.'

Thomas Fiddler's legends and stories were, years ago, told only in the winter time when the spirit world was in dormancy. They were always told but were not depicted graphically. What existed pictorially in boreal culture was limited to rock paintings of animals on various cliff outcroppings where cliff dwellers* lived. Other art forms were designs in dyed porcupine quills woven into clothing, and earlier boreal hunters wore tattoos on their faces and bodies but this art form disappeared sometime in the nineteenth century. What was to remain in a changing boreal culture was for a person to decide to paint episodes from those legends which held the world view of the people of the boreal forest.

Then, just two decades ago, a native man from Beardmore, on the edge of Lake Nipigon, had an electrifying art show in Toronto. His western name was Norval Morrisseau but his boreal name was Copper Thunderbird and he proclaimed himself 'a born artist.' We know from seeing his first works that his proclamation was not quite so. He became an artist quickly but he was not born one in the sense of having adequate technique; nevertheless, his rise into the art world had the rapidity of a shooting star on a moonless night. For the first time a boreal man had emerged from his culture and gained immediate artistic acclaim and a reputation for his eccentricities. Other boreal painters were quick to follow Morrisseau into painting aspects of their ancient culture. It seemed in retrospect that what was a single shooting star was but a prelude to a heavenly shower. Those artists that were mere imitators of Morrisseau fell by the wayside. But two to three dozen artists from boreal culture have entered the art scene since Morrisseau's first show in Toronto in 1962. These artists live by their brushes and knowledge of their boreal culture. In viewing their emergence in an economic way, we see this as the largest and most successful native development for employment in the boreal north – with no government involvement.

Obviously the success of these boreal painters indicates a keen interest in Canada and the western countries in native culture, and this raises an important question. What is it about boreal painting that patrons, collectors and westernized people find so appealing? For boreal art in Canada has found a very wide audience, indeed; policemen, students, construction

---

* Short statured humanoids with hairy faces and no noses. Boreal name: May-may-quay-shi-wok

13

workers, civil servants, teachers and persons of all social strata purchase this type of painting. Perhaps the reason for this popularity is that the art form is highly decorative, colorful and only semi-abstract, where the forms are easily identifiable and directly connected to reality. No doubt the animal life depicted in this art is attractive. Loons, frogs, fish, wolves, moose, mink, foxes, caribou, marten, turtles, snakes are very often the subject matter of this art. In many ways native boreal art is non-realistic wildlife art which is also a very salable art form. Boreal art is also strong in its ecological depiction. Many paintings have 'life lines' that connote the inter-relationships between man and creatures. If the painting is based on an episode from a legend – as the illustrations are in this book – this only adds to communicativeness and consumer appeal. The question 'What is this painting about?' can then be answered very easily for the beholder. Possibly the question of appeal lies in some human traits that are more subtle; this art is mystic, spiritual, even shamanistic, and has ancient cultural roots. The boreal painting by the artists in this book is an attempt to preserve a past that was once vital but is now under alteration. It is, then, art with 'heritage' and is not revolutionary or political like some contemporary art forms. But the base of popularity is in the economics of a product, and boreal painting has had the advantage of being reasonably priced for appreciators. This has made works accessible to people who could not otherwise afford original paintings for their walls. All of these factors, from the content, line and colour of boreal paintings with their heritage through to the purchase price account for the growth of a boreal art that has added a new dimension to Canadian art forms.

Legends of Weesakayjac

THE LEGENDS that eighty year old Thomas Fiddler tells in this first chapter are foundation stories for understanding boreal culture. Foundation because the events in the first three legends occur in the pale before human beings were extant on earth. Only Weesakayjac and the creatures inhabit the forest world. Weesakayjac, who is human in form, is a hunter and he travels with another hunter, his little brother, the wolf. It leads one to conclude that in boreal culture there is a brotherhood between men and wolves. The strength of this bond was illustrated when a pioneer in the 1840s asked why the Indians 'did not kill more wolves as the bounty was so high?' The answer received was 'Indians no care to kill wolves, they hunters as well Indians.'

The bond between boreal folk and the forest creatures extends to more than a common pursuit with wolves. Weesakayjac cooperates with all the creatures and they with him. It is the Muskrat who saves the earth after the flood. It was the lowly Frog who came upon the idea that the boreal forest should have five moons of winter. In the Weesakayjac and other legends that occur before mankind one sees that each creature is endowed with strengths and limitations. It is from these creatures that human beings eventually arrive in the forests. Before Christian concepts had any influence, boreal people believed they originated from certain creatures. These creatures became their clan symbols. Thomas Fiddler is the leader of the Sucker clan. Edward Rae is from the Sturgeon clan; Thomas Linklater from clan Caribou. Other prominent clans along the upper Severn River are the Pelican and Crane clans.

'Every Indian is related to a creature,' Thomas asserted when telling these legends. 'Even when two people who are complete strangers meet but are related to a common creature, they will treat each other like brothers.'

A larger collection of Weesakayjac and creature legends, as in 'Sacred Legends of the Sandy Lake Cree' reveal that the inherent teachings in these foundation stories deal with the polarities of life. Intelligent and stupid; good and evil; feast and famine; malice and benevolence; strong and weak; honesty and deception; Weesakayjac exhibits all of these traits. Unlike the Jesus figure in Judeo-Christian mythology, Weesakayjac is hardly divine in his actions. He is not a puritan and he warns: 'Human beings will act and behave the way I have done.' For this assertion Weesakayjac can be given recognition as a spirit being of humanity who exemplifies the reality of human nature. For those who believe in Weesakayjac, one can hardly find a better teacher on the wild behaviour of human beings.

Weesakayjac in the fourth story of this selection appears after humans inhabited the earth. It is said that Weesakayjac lived in the boreal forest until the whiteman came to the North American continent then disappeared. *–J.R.S.*

WEESAKAYJAC, HIS LITTLE BROTHER WOLF AND THE FLOOD,
DOUGLAS KAKEKAGUMICK

1. Weesakayjac, His Little Brother Wolf and The Flood

Thomas Fiddler

Weesakayjac married a wolf; well, not really married but they were partners. The wolf killed a moose. Weesakayjac agreed they should move their camp to the place where the moose was. At the new campsite, they built a smoke house with a fire in the center and racks above to dry the meat. The moose that wolf killed was really fat. When they finished drying the meat, they took it down from the racks.

Weesakayjac got a bright idea: they would eat the parts of the moose according to their own names. Weesakayjac told his little brother, wolf: 'Because your name is Maeengan, you will eat o'gran, the bones. Because my name is Weesakayjac I will eat the weas, meat, and wee's, the fat.'

So little brother was left with all the bones.

After they finished eating the moose, they started hunting again. They saw the tracks of another moose so little brother told Weesakayjac they would try and kill it. At this time, Weesakayjac did not have a gun, nor did he have the speed to catch up with the moose to kill it. Weesakayjac told his little brother to go on the other side of the lake and start howling so the moose would come his way.

Weesakayjac's plan worked well. When the moose came running, Weesakayjac was concealed behind some brush and he speared the moose as it went by. They followed the same eating plan as before. Weesakayjac devoured all the meat and fat and little brother ate all the bones.

Weesakayjac was always camping with his little brother, but after awhile their food supply ran out. One night when they were sleeping, Weesakayjac began to cry in his sleep. In the morning, wolf asked Weesakayjac why he was crying in the night. Weesakayjac answered: 'You are the reason I was crying in my sleep. I had a terrible dream about you. You were chasing a moose and the moose approached water and you went in the lake after it. When you were half-way across the lake, I saw a swirl of water as you went under and drowned.'

Then Weesakayjac told his little brother never to go in the

water after a moose. 'Don't go after it, even if you are practically on top of it.'

Then wolf went hunting and never came back. When Weesakayjac finally realized his little brother wasn't coming back, he followed his trail. When Weesakayjac was trailing he discovered that wolf had started chasing a moose. Wolf chased the moose down a hill and the moose jumped into the water. Wolf's trail ended at the lake's edge.

Weesakayjac broke off a dead tree limb and threw it into the water. The limb turned into a wolf and it started to swim out on the lake. When the wolf was almost in the middle, the water swirled like a whirlpool. The wolf was carried around and around in it with only his head above the water. Weesakayjac heard him howling: 'Oooooooooooooo!' Thus, Weesakayjac knew his little brother had drowned.

Weesakayjac walked along the shoreline and he came upon a sandy beach that had rocks sticking up through it. There was a dead tree on the beach, its limbs extended above the water. A kingfisher was perched on it.

At this time kingfisher had a bill shaped like a duck's.

Weesakayjac called out to the kingfisher: 'What are you looking at?'

Kingfisher said: 'I'm looking at the small fish in the lake but I can't spear them with my bill.'

Weesakayjac then told the kingfisher that he wasn't really looking at this small fish. If he would tell what he was really looking at, Weesakayjac promised to file down his bill into a spear and to brighten up his feathers.

Kingfisher said: 'It is true I am looking at something else. I am watching the underwater cats playing with the head of a wolf.'

Weesakayjac then asked: 'What will the underwater cats do after they have finished playing their game?'

Kingfisher answered: 'The big underwater cat will get out of the water in the mid-night and sleep on the beach.'

Weesakayjac did what he had promised. He sharpened kingfisher's bill, and brightened up his feathers: a greenish head; a white breast; and a reddish collar. After Weesakayjac did this, he went into the woods to get a big stump, and he hauled it out and placed it on the sandy beach. Then he hid in it.

Weesakayjac had an ice pick with him and towards midnight, he heard the underwater cat crawling out of the water. The leader of the underwater cats was very large and very black. When the ogema came on the beach he noticed the stump and he said: 'That big tree trunk wasn't on the beach when we slept here before!'

But another cat said: 'No. It has always been there since we have been sleeping on this beach.'

They fell asleep shortly after midnight. Then Weesakayjac got out of the tree trunk and speared the leader right through the ribs. The leader screamed: 'Weesakayjac is killing us!' All the cats scrambled into the water, the leader also, with the ice pick sticking out of his ribs.

Weesakayjac went off in the woods. Later he heard somebody coming toward him. This somebody was sort of crying. Weesakayjac went to meet this person who was crying. He saw that it was an old lady. Weesakayjac learned that this old woman was the mother of the leader of the underwater cat that he had speared with the ice pick. The old lady told Weesakayjac that she was looking for wood to build a platform where she would place her son's body when he was dead.

Weesakayjac kept walking and soon he heard another person coming, singing a chant as it came along. Weesakayjac saw that it was a frog that came toward him.

Weesakayjac asked the frog, 'Why are you chanting?'

Frog said, 'I am chanting because Weesakayjac almost killed someone.'

Then Weesakayjac asked: 'What will you do when you get to the place where you are going?'

Frog said: 'When I get there I will be treated well. First, they will give me a meal and lots of fat. And, I have told the underwater cats to build a shaking tent so that I can get their leader to survive.'

Thereupon, Weesakayjac picked up a big stick and clubbed frog, killing him. He skinned the frog and pulled the skin over himself and started off, chanting like the frog.

Weesakayjac went straight to the lodgings of the cats. Upon

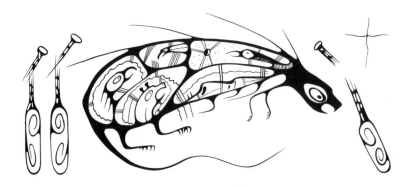

MUSKRAT CHEWS PADDLES, GELINEAU P. FISHER

arrival, they gave Weesakayjac lots of food.

Inside their lodging, the cats had built a shaking tent. The leader lay inside the shaking tent. Weesakayjac then went in there and pushed the ice pick right through the leader, killing him. Then he went out of the lodgings, threw away the frog's skin and walked off.

At the platform they placed the dead leader. Weesakayjac went there and chopped the head off the cat's body. Then Weesakayjac called all the wolves together and presented the cat's head to them so they could play with it. The remaining underwater cats were very angry when they saw this. They sunk the whole earth. The cats told Weesakayjac they would drown the whole earth and that Weesakayjac would drown too. After this warning, Weesakayjac built a big boat. Then he gathered all the animals. Then the rains came. It rained so much the earth was not visible any more. When the rains finally stopped, Weesakayjac called the water animals together. From the big boat, he wanted one of them to swim to the bottom, to reach the earth. The first animal he asked was the otter. He tied a cord to its foot and he told the otter to shake the cord if he was drowning. The otter could not reach the bottom. Next, it was the beaver who tried to swim to the bottom. Weesakayjac tied a cord to him but the same thing happened to the beaver; he couldn't reach the bottom. He failed. Then it was the muskrat's turn. Muskrat went down and down and after awhile Weesakayjac felt the cord shaking. He pulled it up. When he got muskrat to the surface, he discovered that muskrat had drowned. But muskrat had something clutched in his hand. It was a piece of moss, so Weesakayjac knew that muskrat had reached the bottom.

Weesakayjac blew on the moss. 'Pooh, pooh!' The moss began to grow larger. While Weesakayjac blew on the moss, it turned into earth and grew more.

Finally Weesakayjac asked the wolverine to run around this earth to see how large it was. Wolverine ran out three times and each time he came back and said: 'The earth isn't that large yet.'

On the fourth trip out, the wolverine did not come back to the boat and Weesakayjac realized that the earth was now as large as before. Weesakayjac then let all the animals out of the boat.

That's how Weesakayjac made the earth again.

2. Weesakayjac and the Return of Summer

Thomas Fiddler

It happened upon a time there was no summer; the creatures knew that something was holding it back. So, all the creatures on earth decided to have a big meeting to try and find out why summer never returned to the country. All the creatures gathered, and Weesakayjac was present at this meeting where it was decided they would all journey south to find neebin, the summer. Everyone realized that someone or something was holding neebin. They would try to get summer back.

Secretly, Weesakayjac and the creatures journeyed. When they arrived at their destination, they knew exactly where summer was being held captive. But Weesakayjac and the creatures from the north remained hidden. No-one knew they were there.

The creatures who held neebin captive lived in a longhouse.

Weesakayjac and the others had another meeting to decide

who would spy on this longhouse. It was decided a fowl should do this, one who could fly without making any noise. Kookooko'oo, the owl, was chosen.

Owl made no sound. He just stretched out his wings and rose straight up in the air. But, when owl landed and folded up his wings, he made a terrific rustling noise; it was decided that he would not be the spy.

A bird that looks like owl was chosen. He was called 'Cheskihsih.' Cheskihsih couldn't see in the daytime; only at night did he have good vision. That night, Cheskihsih flew over to the lodging and poked his eyes and beak through a knothole in the lodge.

Creatures in this lodge were very cautious. They were sure that sometime, somehow, someone would try to spy on them. One of them in the lodge said: 'What's that thing in that small hole. Is that someone looking in?'

One of the respected creatures in the lodge said, 'Someone should pick up a burning stick and poke it through the hole. If that thing is alive, it will pull its head away.'

One of them held a burning stick to Cheskihsih's nose but he didn't move. After a while the creatures in the lodge agreed, it was nothing. Then Cheskihsih went back to Weesakayjac and the others and told them he saw neebin hanging in a bag in the middle of the longhouse.

Early that evening, Weesakayjac went down to the lakeshore near the village of these people. Just before sunset, he heard the sound of muskrat swimming along the shore. This muskrat was going very slow, because the muskrat had a huge tail like a beaver. He just couldn't swim very fast with that big tail behind.

Weesakayjac called out to the muskrat: 'Little brother, why are you swimming so slow?'

Muskrat said, 'My tail is so big I can't swim any faster.'

Weesakayjac asked muskrat: 'Will you accompany me back to our camp. We will give you lots of food to eat, lots of fats.'

'A-heh!' Muskrat agreed to go.

Weesakayjac also promised muskrat he would narrow out his tail.

Creatures who were holding neebin had a large number of

birch-bark canoes. They had their village situated in a bay, where they could see another small bay, right across from the village.

Weesakayjac and the creatures asked muskrat to go down to these canoes and chew the paddles almost in half and then return to those creatures' longhouse. Muskrat did not enter their lodge until late at night because he was busy doing the chewing chore that Weesakayjac asked him to do. When muskrat entered the longhouse, he was very cold so he huddled close to the fire. Those in the longhouse suspected muskrat of trying to do something against them.

While muskrat was warming up, the fat from the moose he had eaten at Weesakayjac's camp, gave off an odour. The creatures in the longhouse smelled this and they thought some-one had given muskrat something to eat. But, muskrat said, the reason he smelled greasy was he had eaten juicy moose roots from the lake bottom. Muskrat did not want to tell the truth about where he had been; he had to get his tail straightened out.

Weesakayjac, the next morning, went to the other side of the small bay while the others planned to attack the village where neebin was being held in the longhouse.

On the bay shore, Weesakayjac pulled up an old stump which was spread out like antlers. Then, Weesakayjac started swimming across the bay with the stump on his head. In the village, they saw this and they began shouting, 'Look, there is a moose crossing!'

Almost all of them ran to the shore and jumped in their canoes and began to chase the moose. But before they left on the chase, they told two that had loud voices to stay behind and warn them if someone should come to the village. These were O'muckakee, the frog, and Wichijak, the crane.

The creatures from the village chased the moose but they did not quite catch it before it reached the other shore. Meanwhile, the creatures after summer were slowly creeping up on the vil-lage. Then they charged the longhouse. The first creatures to enter the longhouse grabbed crane and started chasing frog, trying to spear him with crane's sharp beak. Finally the creature speared frog, but not before he yelled a warning to the

CARIBOU, GELINEAU P. FISHER

villagers out in their canoes. At that moment, they saw that it was Weesakayjac climbing out on the shore. The creatures in their canoes said: 'There is the frog's warning!! There is an attack on our village.'

They paddled back quickly toward the village but then their paddles all broke in half because muskrat had chewed them.

The creatures inside the longhouse cut neebin down from the place it was hanging and ran outside with it. As they ran along with neebin, the land turned into summer. Leaves burst out on the trees as they passed.

When the other creatures finally got back to their village, they chased after Weesakayjac and the others but they did not catch up to them until they had travelled back into the north. When the villagers reached them, the fisher grabbed the bag of summer and ran to the top of a very tall tree. When fisher was on top of the tree someone shot an arrow at him. The arrow clipped fisher's rear-end. He dropped the bag to the ground and jumped out into the universe where the stars are. They say you can see four stars forming a square in the night time. This is the place fisher landed.

All the creatures there decided to have one big meeting so that everyone could be satisfied with the amount of summer they would get. Everyone could be satisfied if neebin moved back and forth, then all would have an equal amount of summer. They all agreed to do this and they also talked about how many moons there should be in winter.

At this meeting, O'muckakee, frog, held up his hand and said: 'This is how many moons there should be in winter.' One of the important people at the meeting said: 'Frog is getting too bold for his own good,' and then he bashed O'muckakee right across the head. Frog rolled over and his tongue hung out. Then they dragged frog toward the doorway and left him lying there, belly-up.

Then the question was repeated: 'How many moons should there be in the winter?'

The beaver, said: 'The moons of winter should be the same as the number of scales there are on my tail.'

The other creatures said that would be too many moons of winter. In fact, the water would freeze right to the bottom of the lakes if they agreed to that and beaver would die. Beaver's suggestion was refused.

Atik, the caribou, said: 'If you count the hairs in my white collar, that's how many moons there should be!' But this wasn't suitable, because to agree would mean the snow would be so high, caribou wouldn't be able to travel anywhere. They couldn't reach a suitable agreement on this subject.

One of the wise and respected elders got up and said: 'What about the first person who spoke, who had his hand up in the air?' Then this wise elder asked someone to go and count frog's fingers. Then they talked about five moons as suitable for winter, and all the creatures in the meeting held up their hands in agreement that there would be that many moons of winter.

The people at the meeting asked the others to try and bring frog back to consciousness. Weesakayjac was given the task of reviving the frog, O'muckakee. Weesakayjac walked over to the frog and blew on him causing frog to regain consciousness and sit up.

They informed frog the results of their meeting and they asked him if there was anything he wanted to say or do to signify the great event that had just taken place.

'A-heh,' frog said.

Frog had an arrow with three notches on the head of it and

he said he would shoot this arrow up in the sky. When he shot it into the sky, it became a shooting star. Then, frog said: 'As long as my arrow is flying there will be an earth, but should this arrow ever return, the earth will no longer exist.'

On the arrow the frog shot he had painted blue, green and pink in between the blunt heads. When the arrow flashed into the sky frog said, the three headed arrow would penetrate three levels of sky. The arrow did this. This is why we see the rainbow, it comes of O'muckakee's three headed arrow.

This O'muckakee is a big green frog with black spots.

'As many spots as I have on my back, that's how many kinds of medicine I've got,' frog says.

When frog was in the south, he made all kinds of things, canoe paddles, many things. He is always preparing things. And often he knows the answers and can predict the future. Frog goes to the river and gathers medicine. There he takes out birch-bark, separates it, and puts medicine in the folds of bark. That is his medicine.

So, sometimes, it is the lowly like O'muckakee that have words that are more honest. When Manitou picks out a leader, he uses the strongest at times, but sometimes he chooses the lowest one to give the answer.

3. Weesakayjac Gives Birth

Thomas Fiddler

One time Weesakayjac gave the people the impression that he was a woman. He dressed up as a pregnant woman. He made the people think that he was already in labour, giving birth. The old ladies were sitting around him in his tent, ready to help him with birth.

Weesakayjac told the old ladies: 'This child can't be born, it is afraid of old ladies.'

Weesakayjac told the old ladies to go outside for a while. When they went out Weesakayjac had a mink with him all this time. He took it out from under his clothes. When he was

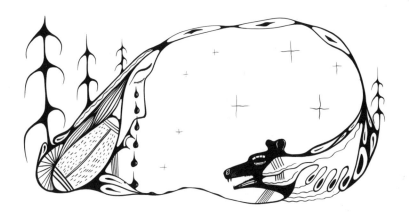

WEESAKAYJAC GIVES BIRTH, GELINEAU P. FISHER

ready, Weesakayjac called out to the old ladies: 'The child has been born.'

He had wrapped the mink in a blanket and was holding on to it. He kept the mink covered up and he squeezed it to make it cry but he didn't let anyone see the baby. He put his baby in a tikanogan. Then he told the old ladies he was going to cut some wood. He put the tikanogan on his back.

Now, a long time ago, women didn't wear panties under their dresses. The old ladies watched Weesakayjac walking up the trail into the forest. While walking this trail, Weesakayjac adjusted the tikanogan on his back, bent forward and his dress went up. The old ladies saw his private parts. They were astonished to see this woman was a man – with a mink jumping out of his tikanogan as he walked away.

Creatures

RESPECT FOR CREATURES by killing them properly and returning parts of their bodies to earth is a strong custom among
clansmen in the forest. This act is spiritual recognition of the
importance of creatures in the lives of men who survived by
hunting them. What is uncanny is the ability of native clansmen to communicate with the creatures by speaking and vis-
ualizing them in the mind. Disturbing as this might be for
persons of western European origin, it is natural for clansmen
since it is already known from boreal mythology that even in
the ancient days Weesakayjac, the spirit being of humanity,
could talk with all the animals. In the four legends that follow, boreal people communicate with moose, bears and
crows. – *J.R.S.*

4. On Killing Moose

Thomas Fiddler

Back in the ancient times, when humans and creatures were living, they stayed in separate places.

These humans had a ceremony with their pipe. One evening, just before they were going out hunting, they lit up their long pipe to smoke.

That evening the moose were sitting in their lodging. There was a big bull moose, some old moose, cows, young ones and a young bull moose around the fire. Suddenly, a pipe came through the opening in their lodging. This long pipe came sailing through the doorway. No one was holding it. It floated by the big bull, the old one, the cows, the young ones. When it reached the young bull moose, he grabbed it and started to smoke on it.

The old moose told him: 'You have destroyed us. This is what the humans do when they are preparing for a hunt. Now, they will be able to get us.'

The next morning at dawn these moose all went outside to eat.

The big bull told the young bull: 'If anyone hears a twig snap, we must run for our lives!'

This same young moose told his mother and father that he could outrun any danger. And he demonstrated by running off, kicking up the snow with his hooves. Then the young moose said: 'I can outrun a wahkahyahpeedaysih, a creature with teeth set all around his jaws.'

Then his mother told him she believed that humans had feathers on their feet. 'They look like they have feathered feet, especially to us; we can't walk on top of the snow.'

At that moment they scented the hunters.

The young moose ran off, alone, he was so certain he could outrun the hunters. While the hunters were chasing them, they saw the young bull stray off from the herd and stand by himself. Hunters ran after the young bull, ran him down and killed him. Hunters also trailed the rest of the herd.

It was in the spring of the year when the snow crust is hard

THE BEARCHILD, DOUGLAS KAKEKAGUMICK

and at the time when cows were carrying calves so they ran slower than the rest. A cow lagged behind and the hunters caught up to her and killed her.

The big bull took off and he ran a long way before the hunters caught and killed him. Now, long ago, there was a saying among the hunters that if you leave the carcass of moose lying around, not gutted and prepared, the spirit being of moose wouldn't like it. So, the big bull ran quite a long way off and the hunters could not return quickly enough to gut him. They didn't touch the carcass until a long time after his killing.

Mysteriously, all the moose that were killed reappeared back in their lodgings. In the morning, the young bull moose awoke and found a musket by his pillow. He inspected it and rubbed the barrel with his hands. The same thing occurred when the cow got up she inspected the musket by her head. But the big bull moose didn't get up early, he slept late into the day. When he did get up, he too picked up the musket and rubbed the barrel. But he had an angry look on his face because his carcass was not prepared quickly.

This is why, close-up, a bull moose always has an angry look on his face!

You should always prepare a creature's carcass right away otherwise it will evade a hunter and not let him kill it.

5. The Bearchild

Edward Rae

Did you ever hear about the time Makwah, the bear, took a little child? A couple of ladies went to pick berries. One put her child asleep and left it. After she finished picking berries she went to check her child and it was gone.

She looked around where she left the child and she saw a fresh bear track going away from this place. She followed the bear track and far away from the place she saw her tikanogan lying on the ground. She looked for blood on the tikanogan and ground but there was no sign of blood.

A search party went out to track the bear and child. The bear went into a burnt area, then they lost its tracks. They came to the conclusion that the bear ate this child and they quit the search.

After they concluded this, they tried to forget the misfortune.

Toward spring, one old man said to the mother: 'I think your child is still living.'

This old man later went walking in the bush and he saw where a bear had raked the bark off a tree. He knew there was a bear around the area. He found the bear and dug it out and killed it. Then he cut up the bear. Next, the old man threw out all the grass in the bear den. When he looked he saw the child sitting there. This child was not able to walk when the bear took it. But now the child could walk and when the child saw the bear cut up it started screaming and crying: 'My Mama.'

The old man took the child home.

The child was really fat and he had good clothes. It was not known how or where the bear got clothes for the child. After the child was taken home he was always crying: 'My Mama.' He would cry himself to sleep still saying: 'My Mama.'

While the child was sleeping, the old people tried to make it forget about its bear mama.

This child when fed wouldn't take any rabbit, meat or fish. He just wouldn't take anything.

Then they asked him what he ate? 'Dried berries and crushed dried fish.'

That's the only thing he would eat.

Then they asked him: 'Where do you get the food you used to eat?'

The child replied: 'I used to get dried berries off her front paws and dried fish off the bottom of her feet.'

They tried to keep the child alive so they caught fish, dried it in the sun and they dried berries and this is the food they gave him.

They made it that way for him, but, eventually, the child started to live like an Indian and ate regular food. He forgot about his bear mother.

6. Crow Visits the North Wind

Thomas Fiddler

CROW IS OFTEN A CHARACTER in legends among the clan people. This bird spends much of its time in the boreal forests and is the first to return as winter wanes in late February. In these two stories, told by Thomas Fiddler and his friend Titus Goodman, crow acts as a messenger for a starving clansman, and as a protector for a man under attack from others. For this latter act of assistance, the crow is punished and we are led to understand why his present colouring is black. – *J.R.S.*

One time a man went out to have his visions and when he was sleeping, north wind came to him. North wind told this man, 'I have sympathy and love for you. If anything should go wrong with you and you need my help, just call upon me.'

Later this man was on the verge of starving due to the bitter cold of winter. When this man was close to death, he called upon crow to go to north wind's place and take a message to him: 'You have promised me sympathy and love and to call upon you whenever I need help and I am upon the verge of starving.'

NORTHWIND AND CROW, SAM ASH

Crow flew off to visit north wind. When crow got close to north wind, it became very cold because of the thick frost. When crow arrived at his destination, he saw a building and he went into north wind's home. Inside, he saw a fire and he huddled close to it to get warm because he was almost frozen. Crow didn't say anything; he wanted to get warm first.

North wind told crow: 'You smell awful, melting by the fire. I want you to go out.'

On the way to the door, crow turned around and said to north wind: 'Here's a message that I bring from the person to whom you gave sympathy and love. He says that he is on the verge of freezing.'

North wind replied: 'Tell him that he is lying. I didn't say anything to him or that I would have pity on him.'

When crow flew back, he told the man: 'The north wind says he didn't say anything to you about having pity on you.'

The man told crow: 'Go back to the north wind one more time.'

Crow answered and said: 'I can't go again because I'm

almost frozen.' 'Go again,' the man told crow, 'because you will benefit if north wind suddenly realizes he has sympathy and love for me.' The man told crow to tell north wind to look toward his door, on its right side, because 'north wind told me to put my hand on the wall to make a print to prove that he has promised.'

THE WHITE CROW, SAM ASH

Crow flew off again because he decided he might benefit. As he flew, the same thing happened, he almost froze as he neared north wind's place. Once there, crow did the same thing. He went in and huddled close to the fire. North wind told crow he was making a nuisance of himself; he must go out of the house. When crow hopped over to the door and was just opening it to go out, he turned and said to north wind:

'I have a further message from this person. He says to look toward your door on the right side to see a handprint. It will prove that you have promised him assistance.'

North wind looked at the wall on the right side of the door and he saw a handprint. 'It's true what this man says,' north wind said, 'I did promise him. Give this man a message. Tell him to prepare a great number of arrows.'

Crow returned and told the man what north wind had said. The man did as he was told. He prepared these arrows and that night he filled up his pipe to smoke. But before he smoked, he turned the pipe toward the north and back again. Then, the man smoked and went to sleep.

At daybreak the man got up and looked outside his doorway because he was expecting something or someone from north wind's promise. The sun was just coming up and the man saw a large herd of caribou coming toward him. The caribou came right up to his door and the man just stepped outside and started shooting them with his arrows. Soon the man became tired from drawing his bow. Finally he quit shooting and the caribou herd was still charging past. That winter the man had enough food to last him. The man and crow ate well. It is said this is the reason crows are always around humans. They hope to get scraps.

7. The White Crow

Titus Goodman

One time a lot of people came and threatened a man. These people that were attacking this man weren't trying to kill him. The people that attacked this man tied him by the legs and arms and put him on a high platform they had built. They just threw him up there. Later, crow came gliding around that platform. At this time, the crow's feathers were all white.

The man that was tied up, check on the platform, started losing his strength from hunger. The man asked the crow to untie him, and in exchange, he would feed crow moose fat after he hunted one. The crow began to pick the ropes off this man; it took the crow a long time to untie the ropes with his long beak.

After crow had the man untied, he saw some old clothes sticking out of the melted snow on the ground. Crow picked out the old clothes, got them loose and shook them. When crow shook the clothes, they turned brand new. Crow did this to everything he saw there: socks, rabbit skin coats, pants. After he shook them, they turned into brand new clothing.

At this time, after the guy was untied, the crow began to notice that his powers were diminishing. It happened that these attackers conjured the crow, so he would lose some of his powers.

In payment for untying this man, crow was given a baby moose; it was right out of the womb. The man threw it on the platform, along with the moose fat he had promised crow. After a time, the people that had tied up the man went out hunting for a big moose. After several days of hunting, they finally caught one. Crow saw them skinning the moose and he hummed with pleasure as he looked at that fat moose. Then crow flew away.

These people took all the meat and bones out of the moose and left the hide, with some people hidden under it. One of the men under the hide held out some fat in his hand.

Next morning, crow came back. He spotted the moose fat and landed on it. One of the people grabbed crow and took him back to camp.

They tied up crow by his feet and let him fly up to the smoke hole in the lodge. And they let crow stay there until he was all black from the smoke. They told crow that if he ever let people go on them again, they would kill him next time. This is the reason we see crow flying around. He hasn't tried anything again.

Duels with Neighbouring Clans

TO THE SOUTH AND WEST of the Severn or Bay River drainage basin live other clan groupings of boreal people. In the last century animosity existed between Thomas Fiddler's people – the Sucker clan – and the clans who lived outside the Sucker territory. These clans were the Loons, to the south and Moose, and Kingfisher clans to the west along the Berens River and the easterly shores of Lake Winnipeg. Outright warfare does not seem to have existed but shamanistic killings between the folk on the Bay River and those from Little Grand Rapids and Berens River appear common. An observation of this friction was made in the 1930s by the eminent anthropologist A. I. Halowell:

> Some years ago several Berens River Indians who were out hunting came upon the traps of an Indian of Sandy Lake. There is no love lost between the people of the Berens River and the Sandy Lake Indians; in fact, no marriages occur between the two groups. One of the hunters, egged on by his companions, defecated on one of the traps. Then he sprung the trap so that a piece of feces was left sticking out. Such an act was an insult to the owner of the trap and a deterrent to any animal that might approach it. It was aggressive because, in addition to insulting the owner, it interfered with the purpose for which the trap was set and menaced his making a living. That the Indian who did it recognized the nature of his act is proved by the fact that he later dreamed that a conjurer of the Sandy Lake Band tried to kill him by sorcery.

Other stories in this volume (those in the chapter on Yorkboat men and on the Heroes) illustrate the conflict between clan people from Deer and Sandy Lake and the hunters from Little Grand and Berens River. Here Thomas Fiddler tells two stories, one is in a humorous vein and in the other a shamanistic killing occurs. – *J.R.S.*

8. Asamojamekun Steals a Sandy Lake Woman

Thomas Fiddler

You will remember a long time ago the people from Little Grand Rapids and the Sandy Lake area used to try to kill each other. Often these men fought duels because of women. This is a story about a guy that tried to steal a Sandy Lake woman.

Some people from Little Grand Rapids were trapping and there were people from Sandy Lake around. Asamojamekun from Little Grand saw a woman. She was another man's mate but Asamojamekun sort of liked her.

In the springtime the man and woman from Sandy were picking up goods from the HBC store in Little Grand. Asamojamekun got there in the afternoon. He left his canoe down on the shore. Then he went to visit this Sandy Lake man that he was going to take the woman from. After Asamojamekun visited the man he went back to the shore to arrange his canoe in order to make a quick get-a-way. Asamojamekun made his canoe ready and took his shirt off.

Asamojamekun said to himself: 'I'm not going yet, I haven't visited enough people yet.'

The Sandy Lake husband knew what Asamojamekun was going to do. When Asamojamekun entered the door, the husband shot his gun right at him but it didn't have any effect. Asamojamekun grabbed the woman by the hand and started for the door. He wasn't able to get away very quickly because the woman was dragging behind. She didn't want to go.

When he got her to the canoe he put her in it but she jumped overboard. Everytime he put her in the canoe she jumped overboard. By the time Asamojamekun got her to sit in the canoe he was mad. He was so mad he threw her overboard and paddled away by himself.

9. Lynxhead Kills a Little Grand Trapper

Thomas Fiddler

This is the story of a man named Lynxhead. He was from Caribou Lake; he was a trapper. There was another man involved in this story from Little Grand Rapids. Their traplines adjoined each other. Always in the winter, when Lynxhead was ready to move out on his trapline, this other man was ahead of him. This happened almost every winter.

'If that guy is going to be there ahead of me I'm going to be very unhappy about that,' Lynxhead finally said.

In this time people were conjuring against one another.

Lynxhead was leaving with his son. When he arrived on his trapping ground, he saw tracks everywhere. Someone had been there ahead of him. Trees had been cut down and a platform had been made with meat – caribou and moose – packed on it.

Lynxhead was mad. He cut lots of wood and piled it underneath the platform. He was going to burn it down to the ground and whatever was on the platform. His son told him: 'It's not right to do that, but, if you have made up your mind, I think we should, at least, take some of the meat, so we can have a fairly good meal.'

So they took some of the meat off – what they needed – and had a good meal. Then, Lynxhead burned the platform and the meat.

They followed the tracks of these strangers. They moved ahead on the strangers' tracks. As they followed, they came across a campsite but the strangers had already gone. They could tell from the camp there were four of them – the stranger and his three sons. The stranger and three sons were out hunting for caribou. Lynxhead knew this.

They followed the tracks of four men and came across a pile of caribou dung. Then they travelled on and they met the first son. Lynxhead asked where the old man was. The son replied, 'He's away ahead trying to locate the caribou.'

Lynxhead and his son kept on going and left the stranger's

44

son behind. Eventually, he met another son and asked him where his father was. The reply was the same: 'He's away ahead looking for caribou.'

Then they saw the third son and asked the same question – he got the same answer.

Finally they caught up to the old man. As soon as Lynxhead was within earshot of the old man, he told him: 'I'm really mad. You are killing everything on my trapline.'

The old man knew he was pretty mad and he walked toward him to shake his hand because it was their first meeting. Lynxhead was so mad he almost did not shake his hand.

The old man said: 'How soft is the stranger's hand.'

Lynxhead said: 'Well this stranger is not very soft, even though he has soft hands.'

They started arguing and belittling each other. They kept this up for two hours. Finally all the sons said: 'I think we should make a fire to keep warm.'

As they made the fire go, Lynxhead, his son, the old man and his three sons had a meal. After the meal, the stranger apologized to him for coming on his trapline.

'I'm sorry for what I have done to you for I am just a hunter myself, trying to survive with my family. To show you how sorry I am, I will give you all the meat on my platform.'

(The stranger insulted Lynxhead because he knew he had already destroyed the meat.)

The stranger and his sons parted there. The man from Little Grand was still mad inside of himself for all the things Lynxhead had said to him. The next spring, Lynxhead's wife got sick because this old man conjured against her. All summer she was sick and in the early fall she was almost dead. All of a sudden Lynxhead loaded his gun one evening. He gave it to his son to go outside and shoot it in the air. He shot it off and came back inside.

He said to his son, 'You missed him. Go out again and try it once more.'

The son went out and shot it in the air again. The son came back in again and Lynxhead said, 'You got him this time.'

Slowly his wife recovered from this time on.

The next fall Lynxhead moved all his family back out to his trapline. He never found anyone or tracks on his trapline. On an evening that fall before, the stranger had keeled over and dropped dead.

Legends of the Yorkboat Men

AT WINDY LAKE* in 1833, six clansmen were recruited to work on the yorkboats out of Oxford House, Manitoba. It was at this time that native clansmen began to man the transportation system of the HBC. Prior to this Orkney and Scot servants of the Hudson Bay Company worked these ungainly boats.

An extensive network of river routes were used to haul supplies to various HBC posts. Supplies were transported up the Rushing River from HBC Albany to Osnaburgh House, Long Lac, and Lac Seul. They were rowed up the Thunderbird River from HBC York Factory to Oxford House, to Island Lake, Norway House and down Lake Winnipeg to Fort Garry. They were also used between HBC Berens River and Little Grand Rapids.

Yorkboats varied in size over the years, the largest up to forty feet long hauling nearly five tons with a crew of ten to portage the goods. Most yorkboats, however, were in the 24-28 foot range, carrying slightly over three tons of supplies. Yorkboats were an adaptation of Orkney vessels, first utilized on the Rushing River in 1746. They had advantages over 'north canoes' in that they carried more weight per man, could sail, and endured rough water that forced canoes to beach to prevent swamping.

Working on the yorkboats often took native men far from their own forest grounds. William McKay, the postmaster at Big Trout Lake in 1855 tells of the experiences of one of his yorkboat crews. All the goods at Big Trout House are brought up by two yorkboats in the late summer from up the coast at York Factory. Early in the summer, not long after break-up, McKay and some hunters from Big Trout Lake leave with the fur bales and go downstream through the Fawn River to the Severn and up the coast to York Factory. But this is a dangerous trip, for it exposes the clansmen to disease outside the boreal forest. York Factory is an international seaport.

* Now called Favourable lake.

And in the fall of 1855, McKay and the boat crews arrive back here at Big Trout much later than usual. Mckay leaves us a description of this journey in his post journal:

'last night I arrived with the two Boats and with my patie (party) all worn oute with Sicnefs, which they caught befor laveing york factory the Influenze two days after leaving York the most of the whole partie were lade upe.'

'I hardly could muster so meney hands as to work the Seals (sails) of the Boats to Severn – I remened at that place Eight days expecting they would recrute their health Instade of that they got worst.'

'In that state I left Severn Three day after one of the partie died, the Steersman of one of the Boats, 4 & 5 of the partie were frequently carried oute the Boats in their Blankets. I left Severn on the 13 August from that time tell I arrived at this place there wase no moar then about one half of the partie that could work, sometimes taking one Boat, and going back for the other this was the case in the rappets or in any strong place.'

'On the 24th I was met by Indians from Trout Lake who assisted us ... they Caught the Infection and they got as bad as the Rest.'

'I had to Remen sometimes two and three days in one incampment, the poor creatures were Reduced to Skin & Bon and some of them did not Recover when they went off to their wintering quarters.'

It took McKay and the yorkboat men thirty seven days to reach Big Trout House from Severn. It is usually a trip of less than fifteen nights.

To work on yorkboats was a gruelling experience. It was back breaking to portage the supplies and the boats. The following observation was made in 1897:

'Portages as long as three miles ... the men had to carry the entire cargo on their backs. A pack strap with a wide zeather band across their foreheads ... with several feet of stout strapping fastened into either side of the band.

For a load, a sack of flour, or other bagged goods, or a box of goods, securely fastened, and rested below the shoulders. On top of this was piled as much as the man could carry ... loads often weigh over two hundred pounds.

Portages ... their narrow beaten paths. The men seldom walk on them. They learned early that it is better to trot ... the trail was damp with their dropping sweat.

As I would sit – that summer only four years ago – awaiting the reloading of the boats, I could hear their laboured breathing long before I could see them.

Where they had to pull the boats ... *esprit de corps was evident* ... I watched each man putting all his strength into pulling his rope. I observed no shirkers.

I learned from one of the Company officials that many men break down and go to early graves.'

Many stories exist about the yorkboat men. Thomas Fiddler and Edward Rae tell four stories but these are not tales of disease or physical hardship, they are stories of humour and shamanistic duels. – *J.R.S.*

10. The Old Man from Big Trout Lake

Thomas Fiddler

It was the time they were transporting goods to Big Trout Lake following the Bay River. They went up as far as James Bay. Everytime they went to James Bay, one of the men usually died and never came back to Big Trout. Men were killed off by evil spells. Many people from Big Trout got the worst of these spells because they lived so close to James Bay. Soon, the Big Trout people were afraid to send their sons and relations to the James Bay area because everytime they went, someone didn't return.

One of the old men from Big Trout – he was small and frail looking – told the men they should take him along on the trip they made every year. The old man went with them and he took along his medicine pouch which held a pipe and tobacco and things that he used for good and evil purposes. Just before they reached James Bay, the old man and the Big Trout people saw a man and his wife hunting along the river. The people in the boats tried to be friendly with this hunter because they were afraid of this man. They wanted to treat him well. They asked this man if they could go ashore, make camp and cook some grub.

Once ashore, the hunter kept looking at this frail old man from Big Trout. The hunter asked them: 'Why do you bring this frail little man along, he can't work or do anything?'

After they finished eating, the old man said: 'Let's wait awhile and smoke.'

They had spread out some canvas and they were all seated on it. The old man got out his pouch and spread his things out on the canvas. The old man who sat beside the strange hunter started filling up his pipe. He filled the bowl three-quarters full with tobacco and the rest with pusagan, the yellow fungus off a birch tree. The old man lit the fungus in the pipe. Holding the pipe out carefully, he turned it clockwise once and anti-clockwise once. Then, while the fungus was still smouldering, the old man held the pipe so the stranger could take the stem in his mouth. But before the stranger took the pipe in his mouth, the old man spilled the smouldering fungus down his open collar and on his chest.

He was trying to get the stranger mad.

The stranger put out the fungus by rubbing it on his chest. Then he went close to the old man from Big Trout and said, 'You almost got me burned!'

The old man said, 'I did that because everytime our young people come this way, your people manage to kill one of us.'

The hunter was very angry. He told the old man; 'Why don't you come back this way next year?' He said this to the old man because he thought he could kill him easily. The hunter also told the old man that when he came back, to bring some sheets of birchbark so he could use it for his lodging. Birchbark is also used to cover corpses in burial.

After this the Big Trout people departed. They loaded up their goods and had been on the river for two days; they began to understand that something was happening to them. It was very disturbing.

When a spell was cast on someone, a shaman's form travelled through the void to reach the person and scare him. When this occurs, the people around usually get dizzy.

After Big Trout people were travelling, they could feel this presence. Each time this form came close to their sleeping places, they would feel dizzy, so dizzy that some of them couldn't help themselves. When all of the men were getting dizzy, they asked the old man: 'What are you going to do about this? You were the one that made the hunter angry.'

The old man replied, 'I will do something.'

That night, it was pitch black. The old man told the men he wanted two arm spans of rope. He took the rope and went out to where there was a noise sounding. When the old man reached the place, there was sudden gust of wind. The wind swirled in circles. A loud noise, like a gunshot rang out and also the sound of a whip cracking. Every time they heard the whip strike, a strange form cried out in pain. As soon as the whipping noise ceased, the wind quieted.

On the third day the Big Trout people went on the river, some relatives of the hunter visited him in his lodge. They found him dead.

11. Wahpeekeeneeseewhy Defeats the Bee

Thomas Fiddler

This is a story of Wahpeekeeneeseewhy. This old man was originally from Sandy Lake.

And during this year, the people are hungry, food was very scarce. An old lady went out at night time to try and catch fish. All she caught was a five inch pike. The old lady who went fishing put it on the ground in her wigwam, which had a hole in the top of it to let smoke out. This man, Wahpeekeeneeseewhy, saw this fish there. He picked it up and threw it out through the smoke hole. Then he went to bed without eating.

Just before dawn, Wahpeekeeneeseewhy got up and went out. It wasn't quite noon when he returned. He had found a bear hibernating in a cave. He carried a sack full of bear meat. They ate pretty well from that meat.

Wahpeekeeneeseewhy was an old man but he could perform miracles.

After this, they went down to Little Grand Rapids and then over to Berens River to get supplies. Just before they entered Berens River Lake, there were houses in sight. They saw this man working outside his house, just planing lumber. When they landed they went up to see this man. Beside his house was a pile of planed lumber. He was planing that lumber because he was going to make a coffin. As he was planing away, he had almost finished the coffin. It was very fancy to look at. He didn't say that someone had died. But they couldn't ask him why he was making it; they felt it was sacred seeing a coffin. And they were afraid to ask him what was the matter.

Just as they were going, one of the men asked: 'You are making that coffin. Who died?'

He said: 'Nobody died, I am making this coffin for myself.'

They were very surprised to see this man working on his own coffin.

After they left this man, they went down to the shore to get their supplies and they met this old man who was feared. He could spell on anyone he didn't like. At Berens River they called him Amoo, the Bee, because he has the sting of a bee. Everytime a stranger came to Berens River, this old man caused trouble. But this old Amoo was always treated nice, the HBC was good to him, the men in the yorkboats paid him because they feared him. Amoo was about eighty years old at this time.

When Wahpeekeeneeseewhy and these people landed, they were making a camp, getting supplies and were just waiting around. As soon as Amoo came, they treated him well. They put food in front of him to eat. Amoo had brought his wife along. The people put a table cloth under the plates of food they were eating. While Amoo was eating, they put sugar on his food to treat him well. Then, while Amoo and his wife were eating, Wahpeekeeneeseewhy just yanked the table cloth and spilled everything on Amoo. Amoo stood up, took his wife's hand and said: 'We should go home.'

Wahpeekeeneeseewhy said: 'Amoo, I dislike you as much as you dislike shit!'

Amoo turned and said; 'Wahpeekeeneeseewhy, I'll come and visit you late in the fall at Sandy Lake.'

Wahpeekeeneeseewhy replied: 'I'll be waiting.'

After this, the people loaded their supplies and they were ready to go. They took their supplies back home. Past freeze-up, when it was safe to walk on the ice, they heard noises coming from the direction of Berens River. It was like a thundering noise, the ground was shaking from the vibrations. The people were getting dizzy from the noise. Soon, the noises came closer and they saw a giant coming towards them. He was slightly taller than the trees.

Wahpeekeeneeseewhy got up, put on his mocassins and dressed himself warmly. He told the people to stay inside, then he went out. When they were about to meet, there was a strong wind, the trees were blowing all over. The sound was loud in thunder and lightning crackled. Soon it was quiet. After quite a while, Wahpeekeeneeseewhy came back in but he didn't say anything. Nothing happened again.

During the winter no one went down to Berens River but in the spring they got ready to go and pick up their supplies again. When they got to the lake where the guy was making the coffin, they didn't see him so they didn't stop because they thought the people might think they had something to do with his absence. When they came back, they learned the man had died.

They went on ahead and landed at the company store to pick up supplies. Wahpeekeeneeseewhy and the crew landed and made camp where they usually did. The Berens River people came to greet them and visit with them.

Wahpeekeeneeseewhy said: 'Amoo is not here?'

They said, 'Last winter Amoo was sitting in his house and suddenly he keeled over dead!'

12. Pascan Takes a Wife

Thomas Fiddler

The leader at Little Grand Rapids was Kichi Mokoman, Big Knife. The next man in charge was Pascan. He was a very strong man. It didn't bother him to carry four loads, four hundred pounds on his back over the portages.

These men travel with the yorkboats.

Kichi Mokoman was mated but Pascan was just a young man. These men turned off the river before Norway House and emptied out the yorkboat. Then they went into the village to choose girls. When they got to the village, the men spread out and started visiting people. Pascan went to visit an old lady and her granddaughter in her lodging. While he was visiting this lady he tried to figure out where her granddaughter slept. Pascan thought he knew where the girl would be sleeping that night.

The old lady suspected something about Pascan.

At nightfall, the old lady and her granddaughter went to bed, except, around midnight, the old woman changed places with the girl. Pascan crawled into bed and slept with the old lady all night. Of course, he did not realize who she was, and he asked her to marry him. She agreed to leave with him on the yorkboats the next morning. Pascan left the lodging before daybreak.

The next morning, Kichi Mokoman and the men were getting ready to leave when all the young men of the village came down and said: 'Hold on. There is a young man who wants to take a wife with him.'

All the important people of the village came down to the yorkboat. Then an old lady came hobbling down. She was leaning on a little stick. As soon as Kichi Mokoman saw her he said: 'Is that the one who is going to get married.'

Then Kichi Mokoman said: 'Push off. There's no young man here who would want to marry an old lady like that.'

They pushed away from shore.

The old lady dropped her stick and began to cry, saying: 'I will always remember the enjoyment I had last night when the young man visited me.'

13. Death at Snake Hill

Edward Rae

This story comes from Island Lake area. They were hauling freight for the store and along the way there is a place called Snake Hill. When these men went through this area, they had to be very quiet, they didn't want the snakes to know they were present. While they were hauling the big wooden boat on this portage near the hill, one young man, a daring type, disappeared. They lost this young man while they were portaging. The leader of this group looked for signs to see where the young man went and the tracks let straight to the place of the big snakes. The young man's tracks led to this big hill where the snakes were bigger than moose. The leader turned back from there because he was certain the young man was going to die or was already dead.

They became sure he was dead so they left and went back home to Island Lake.

At home they told his parents: 'Your boy is gone!' Then, they explained exactly what happened. These parents started crying right away but soon the father suddenly stopped.

He said: 'Why am I crying? No matter how much I cry, my son won't live again.'

He told his wife: 'Stop crying. No matter how much we cry our son won't live. Tomorrow, we will go where our son went; just the two of us. It's better if no-one else dies at that place.'

When they got to the portage where his son was last seen, they made a camp and set up a tent. This father made his tent very strong; staked it all around and tied ropes over the top of it. After, the father went inside and smoked his pipe. He turned the pipe around and talked to the thunderbirds.

Just as the sun was going down that evening, thunder clouds moved in and lightning flashed – the lightning moved toward where they were camped. When night came, the thunderbirds reached them overhead and everything turned quiet.

When the clouds came over Snake hill, lightning started again and it thundered all night long. The mother said: 'During the night the ground shook so much from lightning hitting the snake hill that it almost raised me off the ground.'

In sun-up, all the clouds started to clear and float away. The father and mother took down their tent and went home.

Now, up until this time, people noticed that the snake hill was getting larger and larger every summer.

Later on, this father told his wife he was going back there alone. When he reached the portage, he couldn't see the big hill. It was gone. The area was completely clear of trees. And he saw some huge snakes blown into pieces. He looked for signs of living snakes but all had been destroyed by lightning. He walked all over the place but saw only blood and pieces of snakes.

The father went home. His wish had been realized, no-one would ever die there again.

The people from the main camp never went back to that place for more than two years, the smell was so bad around that portage, they couldn't stand it.

14. Charles Goodman Calls Up The Wind

Thomas Fiddler

THE USE OF YORKBOATS for freighting ended in the early years of the twentieth century. The following story takes place while men are using freight canoes and probably occurred in the 1920s. —*J.R.S.*

When I worked at Caribou Lake, the hardest part of freighting was rowing the canoes. I didn't mind carrying freight over long and rough portages. It was the rowing that was difficult.

When we were freighting from Little Grand Rapids to Caribou Lake, we had to cross twenty-eight portages during a trip which would take at least three days. All of these portages were so long that we would have to stop halfway to rest.

Once we were freighting from Little Grand to Caribou Lake and an old man named Posagee, Charles Goodman, was in charge of twelve canoes and twenty four men. Charles was a brother to me under our custom.

Now Caribou Lake is such a long lake that if we entered the west end in the morning, it was difficult to reach the camps at the other end in one day. At the west end of Caribou Lake, before entering the lake, there are two small lakes, Black Birch Lake and Bare Ass Lake, plus three portages to cross before actually entering Caribou Lake from our camping place on Black Birch Lake. It was quite difficult to reach home in one day from Black Birch Lake. If it was not windy or if the wind blew in the wrong direction, we would not reach the Caribou Lake settlement by the end of the day.

Once, when we camped on Black Birch Lake we built a fire and started to bake bannock. We put on the mosquito nets and were ready to go to bed but the men were still standing around the campfire talking. Some of the men were rolling cigarettes and others were smoking pipes. They decided to collect some tobacco and present it to Charles so that the wind would be blowing on their backs when they got on Caribou Lake the next morning. Then they would sail all the way home that day.

James Campbell, from Cliff Dwellers Lake was the second oldest there and he was asked to present the tobacco to Charles, who was already in his tent. The men at the campfire were very anxious to hear what the old man would say because, if the wind was right, they would all be home the next day and they would not have to paddle either. When James Campbell returned from seeing Charles the men were so anxious, they were about to jump on him and ask: 'What did the old man say?'

Campbell told the men, 'When I got inside the tent with the tobacco, he told me to go and throw it away. But after we started talking, Charles said he would take the tobacco present anyway and he said he would see what he could do.'

The moon was still glowing in the sky when we got up and broke camp in an attempt to reach the Caribou Lake settlement. The water on Black Birch Lake was very calm and there was no wind at all when we started out. While we paddled along, sporadic but light gusts of wind came from behind us. We crossed the first two portages and stopped at the last portage before entering Caribou Lake to have lunch. Here the men asked James Campbell to approach Charles to ask him if they should put up their sails. Campbell returned and said, 'Fix them anyway.' The men got busy and put up the sails quickly.

Then the men paddled out of the river into the lake. When they reached the mouth of the lake a big gust of wind hit the sails and they started sailing down the lake. When they had sailed half-way across Caribou Lake they started getting hungry. When everybody reached the shore the wind died out and stopped. When they started out again after their meal, Charles advised them that the wind would be returning.

When they put into the lake, the wind returned just as strong as before. As the canoes approached the straight called, 'Little Bear,' from which they could see the settlement, the wind faded away.

Charles told the men: 'Your tobacco presentations have run out!'

But it wasn't that far and we all paddled home.

Heroes from the Past: The Old Young Lad

WISKEHNEEGEE, YOUNG LAD, exists in several legends told by Thomas Fiddler and his friends. The evidence is that he was a hunter in the Crane Clan of Indians along the Severn or Bay River. A 'Wooskeeneekee' traded at Osnaburgh House in the 1820s and an earlier reference in the journals is to a 'Wiskeenick' who was a goose hunter at Fort Albany on the Hudson Bay coast in the 1770s. A later reference (1834) in Hudson Bay journals refers to a hunter from the Red Lake district who was called 'The Little Boy.' Some of these early clansmen are no doubt the flesh and blood origins of this man, whose powerful exploits and invulnerability are remembered in legend. – *J.R.S.*

15. Young Lad and Man Always Sitting Duel with the Little Grand Shaman

Thomas Fiddler

I remember a story that occurred in the days of my grandfather's father.* Jack Fiddler** was only twelve years old when this happened. Their family was living with some others on Setting Net Lake, where the men from our camp would go camping. They would travel as far away as the Caribou Lake area.

The people from Little Grand Rapids would come up and trap in the Caribou Lake area as well. It was late in March and there were three hunters from Little Grand, trapping around Apps Lake which is south of Caribou. Jack Fiddler's brother and his wife were trapping there also. These people did not see each other's tracks in the snow.

At this time, Indians have power – the three men from Little Grand had visions in their dreams and they knew this man and his wife were camped nearby. So they thought about this woman and they conjured to make her visit their camp. These Little Grand conjurers tried to get ahead of this man and make the first trail across the ice before the man could come to the lake.

When Jack's brother and wife started off from his camp, her mind was possessed – she had to visit their camp. As they reached the shoreline and were going up in the bush, the woman told her husband to go ahead, she would follow along behind on his trail. When her husband was out of sight, the woman went back out on the lake and followed the trail of the three Little Grand men who had passed by that morning. The three hunters knew the woman was following them so they went to the other side of the lake and made a new camp. The woman reached them at their campsite.

When the man realized that his wife should have caught up with him a long time ago, he turned back and he found her trail

* Porcupine Standing Sideways, Thomas Fiddler's great grandfather
** Jack Fiddler, Thomas Fiddler's grandfather

63

DUEL WITH THE GRAND SHAMAN, NOAH SAINNAWAP

following the trail of the three men. But he did not have the courage to follow his wife to the camp of the trappers from Little Grand because he knew they would kill him. Disappointed, he returned to his own camp. These three men took the woman back to Little Grand Rapids.

Now the leader of these men was a powerful man called, Neejabesees. After two years, Neejabesees came back to Setting Net with his new wife to visit her relatives. Neejabesees was very confident of his powers and though there were many people who would place revenge upon him, he was certain there was nothing they could do to harm him.

To show his power and confidence Neejabesees tested his strengths before he left Little Grand. He had ordered people to shoot him with their flint locks. When they did this, Neejabesees remained standing, only powder burns showed on his clothes. Neejabesees was highly respected by the Little Grand people because of his invulnerability to threat.

Neejabesees told his people that when he reached Setting Net, he would chant and beat his drum for ten days and nights without rest. He claimed also that he would completely over-power the men in the camp at Setting Net and dispose of them. Neejabesees wanted to get rid of the men because he would then take his choice of the women. He would take ten women back to Little Grand Rapids and give them away as presents.

When Neejabesees arrived at Setting Net, he carried his marten furs, drum, and his captured wife walked with him. He started beating his drum, but there was no way Neejabesees could chant and drum for ten days without stopping. The powerful old medicine men from Setting Net conjured against Neejabesees as he chanted away and soon he was defeated. He had to stop chanting long before the ten nights and days had passed.

When Neejabesees realized that he had been defeated by the shamans at Setting Net, he moved across the lake and camped at the narrows at the north end. After they set up camp, Neejabesees gave the woman his furs and told her to return to the Setting Net camp and trade them for gun powder and lead. He also told her that his intention was to shoot every person at the camp on Setting Net.

When the woman reached the camp, she told her relatives what Neejabesees had said, so the people decided to keep his wife in their camp. During the night, Neejabesees realized that his wife had told the people what he was going to do.

On Setting Net Lake the snow had melted away under the warm sun and the surface glared with bare ice. As soon as the powerful Neejabesees stepped on the ice, his footsteps thundered. The ice cracked beneath him as he walked toward their camp.

The shamans of the Setting Net camp sat in their longhouse. All the other people in the camp hid in the forest in order to escape the oncoming Neejabesees. In the longhouse, the shamans waited, ready for the powerful intruder from Little Grand Rapids.

As Neejabesees neared the camp, he heard the women and children running off in the bush. When Neejabesees got near the door of the longhouse he acted innocently. He talked loudly, so the men inside could hear him: 'What is the matter, are some Indians attacking?'

Then he laughed.

Inside the long birch-bark dwelling a bucket of water hung on a wooden hook. Neejabesees knew the men inside were ready for him, but he strode through the door fearlessly and took the water bucket from the hook. He gulped down the whole pail. While he drank, his eyes scanned the occupants of the longhouse. Then the shamans grabbed him while he was drinking and held him there. They had already planned that they would shoot him. But, first, they staked him to the ground with rope to await his doom. Neejabesees realized that they were going to shoot him.

The Setting Net shamans had made powerful medicine for a special bullet which would kill the attacker. The captors kept the flintlock hidden from Neejabesees so he would not see the instrument of death until the moment it was fired. But Neejabesees knew that he was going to be shot by a gun and he conjured one of the ropes on his leg to fall off and it unravelled and fell away. When they armed the flintlock, Neejabesees kicked the gun out of the way; it fired, sending the bullet to the ground.

Their plan having failed, the Setting Net people tried to beat the man to death, they kicked and punched him but they could not kill him. They even struck him with axes but this assault had no effect.

Finally they cut off Neejabesees' head, then they sliced the rest of his body into pieces and threw the bloody parts of his body through a hole in the ice on the frozen lake.

The people knew this story well, because my grandfather, Jack Fiddler, being only twelve years old, was not frightened by what was taking place. He was playing around with his bow and arrows, watching the sky, singing as he ran around.

The shamans of Setting Net kept a close watch over the hole in the ice because they could hear something chanting at that place. When they checked the hole, they saw Neejabesees, sitting there, completely re-embodied in human form. Someone, the Setting Net men thought, must have given him new power to perform this amazing act. They threw Neejabesees under the ice and then conjured that he would not reappear on the ice

66

again. After that, Neejabesees did not come back to surface.

When summer came, the people at Little Grand Rapids realized that the powerful Neejabesees had been killed by the people at Setting Net.

In the spring, the camp of people at Setting Net moved back to Caribou Lake.

That spring, the old people at Little Grand Rapids tested their shamanistic powers by making medicine salve that could withstand bullets. The salve, when rubbed over their bodies, gave them protection from any assault.

But the men at Caribou Lake had constructed a shaking tent, and a piece of tin was placed inside it. The tin reflected the activities of their enemies even though they were hundreds of miles away. The people at Caribou Lake were thus able to watch the medicine powers that the conjurers at Little Grand Rapids were obtaining. The man in the shaking tent not only saw but heard what the hunters at Little Grand Rapids were saying and he repeated it for his listeners at Caribou Lake. The shaking tent was their way of watching the action of their enemies.

Then, the men in the shaking tent informed the Caribou Lakers that the people from Little Grand were heading out toward them in ten canoes. The Caribou Lake people became frightened and they loaded their canoes and left for Sandy to try and escape their attackers.

At Sandy Lake, an old man lived – it was said that he was over two hundred years old – who was called Wiskehneegee, the Young Lad. They hoped Old Young Lad would offer them protection from their attackers. Wiskehneegee was called, 'Young Lad,' because he was so old and yet he hadn't aged. They say that he did not die from old age, he just got tired of living and gave up.

The Sandy Lake and Caribou Lake people formed together against the people from Little Grand.

When the ten canoes of men from Little Grand reached Caribou Lake and found the encampment deserted, they knew that the Caribou Lake people had fled to Sandy Lake and joined with the people there. But the Sandy Lake and Caribou

YOUNG LAD GETS MARRIED, NOAH SAINNAWAP

Lake group moved up to the east end of Sandy Lake and camped above the great waterfalls – Owepecheewepawetik, the Goldeye Falls.

Now the two groups tested each other's powers by conjuring. Each against the other. They watched the movements and thoughts of each other.

At the new encampment of the Sandy Lakers and Caribou Lakers above the waterfalls, Young Lad asked two men to take him down river, to the place where the water started to sweep away over the falls. When they reached the swift water, Young Lad spread a blanket on the water and stood on it as it swirled through the rapids to the water falls. Then, they saw Young Lad standing on a rocky point below. They blazed marks on two trees to prevent the medicine men from Little Grand accomplishing the same powerful feat because they would have visualized his amazing act. They did not know, however, the blazed trees would prevent them from doing the same thing.

The old leader, Asamojamekun, the brother of the man, Neejabesees, realized that Young Lad was testing his powers and he realized he would have to perform the same magic. He was certain he could do it. But Young Lad knew that once the medicine man tried the same act the blanket would fold over him and snare him inside it. He would, in effect, be wrapped up in a bag. (Not that there was any bag, it was all in the thoughts of Young Lad.)

As soon as the Little Grand warriors reached the falls, Asamojamekun went over the falls on a blanket. In the meantime, the Sandy Lake people moved five miles down the river from the falls to a creek called Ocheekaouwenent. The Little Grand people camped at a place on the Severn River called, Ayecheena Weeseepe. Both parties knew where each other were camped.

The Sandy Lake group leader decided they would make their stand at Ocheekaouwenent. At this place, there were two small rivers going into the Severn River. Their encampment was on a small point, on a little hill. The leader of the Sandy Lakers instructed the people to make a clearing and they dug pits to fight from. Rifle racks were constructed along the pits as ordered by their leader. All the guns were placed in the racks by each pit. The guns were not to be loaded. Their leader told them that when the attackers arrived, all they would have to do would be to pick up their guns, and start shooting. It would not be necessary to load them. Old Young Lad had great power in order to work this feat against the enemy.

Both parties constructed small tents, something like a shaking tent. And they fought each other by conjuring missiles to fly through the air at each other's camp. The pellets that flew towards the Sandy Lakers did not hit anyone, they were attracted to a bowl inside the tent. The Sandy Lake people were not trying to kill anyone, they were just defending themselves.

The Little Grand hunters soon knew that the pellets they conjured to kill the Sandy Lakers were having no effect. Now the distance from the two groups was about six miles; but the river flowed toward the Sandy Lake encampment.

A man called N'jaysup, the Man Always Sitting, in the Sandy Lake camp, operated their shaking tent to see what the Little Grand people were conjuring next. Man Always Sitting told them the Little Grand shamans were sending bad medicine down the river toward their camp. Then Young Lad told the people to fill their buckets up with water and to bring them up to the encampment. This would prevent them from running short of good water. Man Always Sitting was not in the small shaking tent. He sat in his own wigwam beating his drum. He had some birch-bark and he tied it on the end of a stick. He had told the people they would see the bad medicine coming down river in a greasy slick. He sang away and beat his drums, while looking for bad medicine to appear on the river. As soon as the bad medicine reached their camp, he threw down his drum stick, picked up the stick with the birch-bark on it and lit it on fire. Then, Man Always Sitting ran down to the river with the burning torch and threw it into the water. When the torch hit the water, the bad medicine caught on fire and burned across the surface of the river.

For the next three days, pellets flew into the camp of the Sandy Lakers but had no effect.

One of the old people of the Little Grand Rapids people got up early the next morning. He advised his people that he had had enough and he was going to return home. He told his

70

people that, in a vision he was told if they attacked the Sandy Lakers, every one of them would be killed. 'Maybe we will kill some of them but everyone of us will be killed, not one of us will be left!'

Asamojamekun was crazy with revenge because of the death of his brother and he replied; 'Why don't we go ahead and attack anyway?' But the old man did not pay any attention to the words of Asamojamekun. He packed his belongings, got in his canoe and paddled up the river, heading home to Little Grand. Soon all the other men followed and they too returned toward Little Grand. Only Asamojamekun remained, full of hatred. But after a day alone in the camp, he saw that a single-handed attack would be futile. He gave up and paddled off to Little Grand.

After this incident the story went out that the Sandy Lake people were very powerful.

16. Young Lad Attacked by Yorkboat Men

Thomas Fiddler

This man, Young Lad, lived for about two hundred years. His limbs never got old. When he was living he always looked the same. For this reason they called him Wiskehneegee – Young Lad. He never seemed to age. I will tell you a story about him. This happened in the time they used the Yorkboats to get supplies from the James Bay area. At this time, they used to haul lots of fire water. They used to haul barrel containers and they weighed about four hundred pounds. They did not pick up these barrels or haul them on their backs; they usually rolled them.

Young Lad and other Indians usually had plenty of whisky at this time. These Indians tried to get Young Lad drunk so they could stab him with their daggers. They drank lots of whisky and the other men on the Yorkboat got very drunk but Young Lad stayed sober. When they attacked Young Lad with their daggers it didn't even bother him.

I heard people tried to do many bad things to Young Lad. They were jealous because they could not do anything to him. People even tried to kill his children to make Young Lad suffer. But Young Lad did not get into fights or things like that first.

YOUNG LAD ATTACKED BY YORKBOAT MEN, SAM ASH

17. Young Lad's Daughter Gets Killed

Thomas Fiddler

Once Young Lad's daughter married a man. In those days they had longhouses but Young Lad had a small wigwam of himself. In the longhouse where the other people were living, Young Lad's daughter was stabbed to death by her husband. A man came and told Young Lad: 'Your daughter got killed.'

Young Lad got up and took off his shirt and pulled out his knife and went to the longhouse. When he went in there, he said: 'Who's the man who wants to fight with a knife. Let him fight me!' They had prepared for Young Lad's arrival and when he entered, they began to shoot him. At close range the bullets did not have any effect on him; the bullets did not reach him. They tried to stab him but they couldn't penetrate his skin.

The husband did not try to run away, he crawled under a blanket and hid in the longhouse.

Then Young Lad said: 'Who was the man that killed my daughter?'

The people were afraid of Young Lad so they told him: 'There he is beneath that blanket.' He went over and took the blanket away.

'Stand up, we'll fight,' he told his son-in-law.

Then Young Lad grabbed his son-in-law by the hair, stabbed him in the heart and threw his body away. This was the way they treated Young Lad while he was living. All his life they tried to make him feel bad by killing his children or assaulting him. People were very jealous of him because he had lived so long.

18. Young Lad Under Attack

Edward Rae

People tried to kill Young Lad during his life but he never started a fight with any person. Once Young Lad was angry though, he could kill a person right away.

One time, Young Lad and his wife were in camp and just before he went to sleep, he was sitting by the fire getting warm. A man rushed in and shot him in the back. Old Young Lad reached around and felt his back and saw a little bit of blood on his hand. He jumped up – mad – and ran outside after the man. He caught the man, beat him up and killed him. Then, he just tossed the man's body away. When he came back inside, he told his wife to look at his wound. His wife told him there was just a little red spot on his back.

'Huh!' Old Young Lad said, 'I thought he got me that time.'

Then he was sorry that he killed the man.

YOUNG LAD DECIDES TO DIE, NOAH SAINNAWAP

There was another time Young Lad and his wife were out camping some place. They had a caribou hanging up in their camp. That night, someone threw a big rock on him and it broke his leg. The leg bone was sticking out of the flesh. That night before sleep, Young Lad told his wife: 'Cut off the caribou's leg, give it to me, then help me outside.'

Shortly after Old Young Lad was outside, his wife could hear him shouting in the bush. Then she heard him singing but his voice came across the sky above her. He was gone for three nights before he returned. When he came back his leg was completely healed. There wasn't a mark on his skin but all his clothes had faded to white in colour.

19. Young Lad Decides to Die

Thomas Fiddler

Jean Baptiste Fiddler often told this story to me. It was the time that Old Young Lad was going to die. His wife wasn't there when he died but his daughter was. This happened close-by to O'pasquiang Lake. It was in the late fall. His daughter was taking care of him. Young Lad was sitting there. All of a sudden, he said: 'I am tired of life.'

He told everyone – so all would hear – that he was tired of living. He talked to all the people before he died and told them not to harm others, not only his children, but all the people there. He told people if they harmed others they wouldn't live a long life. He lay down and pulled a blanket over his face and died. After about fifteen minutes he told them to pull the blanket from him. He moved his arms and said: 'I forgot to take my little object.'

He told his daughter to pick it up. It was something that looked like a little metal container; small; he always had it. He had something in it. His daughter picked it up from under his pillow and gave it to him. Young Lad unbuttoned his shirt and put it on his chest. Again he pulled the blanket over his face, and finally, Old Young Lad died.

Man Always Sitting

NEEJAYSUP, the Man Always Sitting, is another hero from the past in the legends of the people from Sandy and Deer Lakes. There is some evidence in Hudson Bay journals to substantiate that Neejaysup was a man of flesh and blood who lived in the late eighteenth and early nineteenth centuries. Hudson Bay traders wrote a shortened version of his name in their journals as Assup. Reference to Assup is found in John Kipling's 1786 journals at Gloucester House on the Rushing River. This reference to Assup concerns another clan leader, Jecob* who often supplies the *HBC* traders with caribou, sturgeon, winter fish, and geese. Jecob comes into Gloucester in 1786. He is filled with a deep grief and bitterness. He talks for a long time with Mr. Kipling and later Kipling writes in his journal:

February 23, 1786

'at 11 a.m. came in Captn Jecob and family 6 in number ... he gives me the Malencholley account of his finding one of his daughters in the woods almost naked and froze to death she had been some time wife of a son of Captn Assup who it seems had beat her in a cruel manner strip'd and turn'd her a drift ... Jecob says he will revenge his daughters death and bad usage.'

Then Jecob confronts Assup, in a duel of powers. Jecob, who hunts around Makokibatan Lake guides an attack upon Assup. So in the spring after Jecob's daughter was killed, Assup hunts near the Rushing River, carries his furs and the furs of the other hunters of the Winisk Country down to Fort Severn, instead of to Gloucester House. The trader at Fort Severn wrote saying, Assup:

---

* The descendants of this man, the Jacob family now live in the village of Webequie on the Winisk River.

'came here 31st of last Month with 5 Canoes and traded
183 Made Beaver most of which he got from Weniscau
River Natives who are afraid of him as he is looked upon
as a God. However, I say and often have said he is a pirate
so he makes a common practise of either taking away
Natives or their Goods.'

Jecob, in his duel with Assup, has difficulty with his own
strength. In the mid-winter of 1788, he is 'exceedingly ill.' The
following summer, he sadly canoes to Gloucester House to
bury one of his young hunters who has drowned. The following year, Jecob's family do well and in the spring of 1790 his
men kill ten caribou on one hunt. But Jecob has not avenged
the death of his daughter and Assup again frequents the
Gloucester House with impunity. Then Jecob finally strikes
Assup down: 'arrived here Captains Assup, Atifs and Gangs
eight canoes but poorly gooded partly owing to Assup having
been almost torn to pieces by a Black Bear, in the spring, of
which wounds he is still very ill.' It takes Assup, the shaman, at
least a year to recover from the onslaught of Jecob's mark
because on the next journey to Gloucester he is only 'near well
of wounds received from the Bear last summer.' Other evidence in Fort Severn journals states that the 'Great Northern
Capt. Assup' has left the Rushing River and Winisk River areas
to join the 'Severn Indians.' This is likely the reason that
legends at Deer Lake and Sandy Lake on the upper reaches of
the Severn River are told about Neejaysup, or Assup, the Man
Always Sitting. – *J.R.S.*

MAN ALWAYS SITTING, LEVIUS FIDDLER

20. Man Always Sitting Married a Little Grand Woman

Edward Rae

There was a man from around here in the old days named Man Always Sitting. He used to travel back and forth to Little Grand Rapids and he fell in love with a woman there so he got married over there. The Little Grand Rapids people were revengeful after one of their men had been killed by our people and they decided to kill Always Sitting to even things up. The Little Grand men held a meeting in a tent where they loaded a gun up and asked Always Sitting to come and visit them. As soon as he entered the tent, one man reached for the gun. Always Sitting sprang backwards out of the tent and by the time the Little Grand men got out of the tent, he had disappeared. He moved like lightning. Well, he wasn't that fast but he had disappeared even though they could see his tracks going straight across the lake. The Little Grand men followed Always Sitting's trail to a place where he had spread gunpowder across his tracks. When the Little Grand men saw that gunpowder, they just gave up and turned around.

Always Sitting left Little Grand Rapids without any food or a gun and when he arrived in Deer Lake he was still in good health. Always Sitting was separated from his wife and she cried a long time but he wouldn't go back to Little Grand Rapids because he felt he might be killed for certain.

21. Man Always Sitting, The Beaver Hunter

Edward Rae

Always Sitting was a great medicine man. He could pick up red hot coals from the fire and later he would put them back and there wouldn't be any marks on his hands. When a man was sick, he would grab the man, then open up his hand, holding the objects that made the man sick.

Once a man came in and said he was going to shoot Always

Sitting. He just took his shirt off and said: 'Go ahead, shoot me!' The man shot and it didn't even hurt Always Sitting. There was only a small black dot where the bullet had hit him.

One time, a man told Always Sitting: 'Why don't you go over and kill some beavers in that lake?' The next day, Always Sitting went to the lake and he did not catch any beavers. He got mad. He put on a skunk skin hat that he wore when he beat his drum. He started singing; he was mad that he hadn't caught any beaver. The next morning he went to the lake and killed all the beavers in it. When Always Sitting got mad, he got all kinds of help from his spiritual protectors.

BO-KWATCH-IKWAY AND ALWAYS SITTING, LEVIUS FIDDLER

22. Man Always Sitting Travels with Bo-kwatch-ikway

Edward Rae

Bo-kwatch-ikway was a beautiful and gorgeous woman. When a man made love to her, she would have a child right away. Someone saw Always Sitting with this woman. Of course, he was married and sometimes he would be gone for a month and his wife didn't know he was with Bo-kwatch-ikway during his travels. This time, Always Sitting was with his wife and he started leaving her. First, for one day. Next, he was gone two days. Then, he was away for three days. After he was gone for three days, his wife began to wonder what he was doing. She walked out on a point to look for him. She saw him in a canoe and he was with a beautiful woman all dressed in red clothes. Always Sitting's wife stopped looking and turned away. When she turned around again, her husband and Bo-kwatch-ikway were in the channel beside her. Again she saw the beautiful Bo-kwatch-ikway and Bo-kwatch-ikway saw her. Then, in the wink of an eye, Bo-kwatch-ikway was gone. Her paddle had dropped into the water. Always Sitting turned around to see what had happened and he saw his wife on the shore.

After this, Always Sitting's wife knew what was going on. He told his wife that he had three children by Bo-kwatch-ikway. He just quit travelling with Bo-kwatch-ikway after that. Bo-kwatch-ikway was always jealous of a man who got married.

My father said he travelled with Bo-kwatch-ikway but they never had any children. He already had two wives and he didn't want three!

23. Man Always Sitting, The Beaver Hunter

Thomas Fiddler

The Big Trap, James Meekis, said this story happened when he was young, and I learned it from him. It was in those days when there were no traps like we have now. A hunter, when he

83

MAN ALWAYS SITTING IN LONGHOUSE CEREMONY,
LEVIUS FIDDLER

wanted to get beaver, would find a place where a pond was frozen solid; there was no place for beaver to get out. The hunter would find a hutch and tear it up and kill the beaver. But the beaver usually have their homes quite a distance from the shore and usually there is a path under the ice that isn't frozen so the beaver can get out of the hutch by swimming away.

If this man I am talking about, Man Always Sitting, knew where a beaver was, he went to the hutch and chopped the ice away. When he finished making a hole, he tasted the water. When he tasted the water he could tell if the beaver had passed by, or if the beaver was still in the den.

Always Sitting knew all about beavers.

This story I am telling happened sometime in the fall. The ice had not frozen but freeze-up had started. Always Sitting wanted to catch some beavers for soup and he asked Big Trap to go out hunting with him.

When they found a beaver pond, they sat around waiting for the beaver and it became late evening. The beaver did not come up; not even one beaver came up and night was approaching. It was dark. It got so late, they turned around and paddled home. On their way, Always Sitting said, 'The beavers have a will of their own. I will talk to the great spirit leader of beavers.' While he was talking, he began to sing and chant in Indian as he was paddling. They went home and went to sleep.

The next day they waited until evening and he asked Big Trap to go with him again. They went to the beaver pond and the sun started down. They went on the dam and waited for beavers. All of a sudden, a big beaver came to the surface. Always Sitting fired at beaver and killed it. The flow in the pond carried beaver right up to where they were sitting. It wasn't long before another big beaver surfaced; Always Sitting shot it and the same thing happened again, it floated up to them in the current. After a short time, another beaver came to the surface; this one was smaller in size. He shot it and it floated to him. Always Sitting shot eight beaver there – two big beavers and six small ones. He killed all beaver that were there.

24. Man Always Sitting Leads the Wabino Ceremony

Thomas Fiddler

It was in the time people used to gather at Mud Lake; they used to build a ceremonial longhouse there called the wabino-gamick. Man Always Sitting was a leader, a wabinowin, of this ceremony. This longhouse had one pole up at each end of it. The bark was taken off the poles and one pole had a big boulder beside it. Always Sitting sat in the longhouse and beat his drum.

He had a type of owl, the kind that eats little birds. He got this owl someplace, skinned it, and mounted it on a little pole. While he was beating and singing to the spirits on his drums; suddenly, this owl began to float through the air and land on the big pole at the other end of the longhouse. The owl didn't even flap its wings, it glided through the air. It floated right across to the other side, to the pole.

These ceremonies used to continue for about a week and they had feasts. They killed lots of meat and prepared it, dried it. Then, when this ceremonial came around, they had plenty of food on hand.

Inside the longhouse, on each side of the house, the people sat on blankets but there was a clearing right around the poles where they danced. When they were eating, a man took a dish around and everyone took food from it. They had cut the food into pieces and if one piece dropped to the ground, they didn't like that because the food was sacred.

When Always Sitting was leader, if someone dropped food to the ground, he would beat on his drum to make people look for it. But he had his eyes closed while he beat on the drum, then he would point to the piece of food that had been dropped. The people would find a piece of food way over at the other end of the longhouse. If people couldn't see the food, Always Sitting would say: 'It's over there!' Still no one could find it. When this happened he stopped beating the drums, got up, and went over and picked up the food.

This is a story I heard about Man Always Sitting when he was leading the longhouse ceremonies.

The Marten: James Linklater

'IF YOU THROW ME TO THE GROUND,' the Marten told a man from Berens River, 'you will see sparks of fire.' James Linklater, the Marten, is a contemporary hero in the pine forests. Born late in the nineteenth century, Marten resided at Cliff Dweller Lake and he was for many years the leading headman of the families there. He passed away in 1975. Prior to this demise he told the artist Norval Morrisseau, 'When I leave my people I will be going to live with the cliff dwellers (may-may-quay-shi-wok) and people can come and visit me in the cliffs.' The powerful Marten was known to carry as part of his shaman's tools, a tiny silver bottle which held a powerful medicine as well as a book of undecipherable writings through which he communicated with the spirit of a white woman. To Thomas Fiddler and others, the Marten was a man to be given much respect for his curing abilities; abilities that were in the eyes of many, heroic. –J.R.S.

25. Marten Cures Thomas Fiddler

Thomas Fiddler

When I was young, seventeen winters, and we were living in the bush about forty miles from Caribou Lake, I accidentally cut my leg with an axe while setting a trap. It was in the month that crows return. I did not cut the bone but the flesh below my knee; the side of the skin was cut away. Two days after the accident, the wound began to affect me and I became very ill. I was really sick; I think the people were very sorry – unhappy about it.

There were many older people who were healers, or medicine men, who went into the shaking tent to try and cure the infection in my leg. One of the older medicine men, tried in the shaking tent to cure the infection in my leg. Finally, he said: 'I can't help you.' No matter how many people tried to cure me with the shaking tent, it did not make me better. I was lying flat on my back, my leg was swollen up badly. I had been sick many days; the geese were flying north.

Then Marten came from Cliff Dwellers Lake to the place where I was ill. The people put up a lot of stuff to pay him: guns, clothes, and tobacco. So Marten said he wanted to look at my leg, so he could see through it. At this time I could hardly even move my head around. While I was lying there, they built a shaking tent. Marten went in and the tent began to shake. When the tent stopped, Marten said he was told he should know what to do because there were bugs in my leg. Then he began performing the tent over again. He wanted a lot of wind to enter the tent so he left the door open to let the spirits enter. When the tent began shaking violently, Marten shouted: 'Come in!'

As this happened, I saw something going in the tent. A voice sounded out of the tent, saying: 'I am a metal insect!' Then the tent stopped.

Marten came out and told the people they should get a white cloth – a real white cloth – and wrap it around my leg. They washed my leg down; they put on that white cloth and covered it up. Then they told Marten they were finished.

MARTEN IN CANOE, JOHNSON MEEKIS

This thing, that went into the shaking tent, began to sing again. Marten said: 'Beware of me!' It was a warning so the thing would not get startled or frightened.

Now, of all the people that had come around to try and heal me – I didn't really think anything would happen. Then the thing that went in the tent came out and came down toward my leg, it made a whistling sound as it came on. As it approached a shock went through me from head to my toes. The shaking tent stopped. A little while later, Marten's voice said: 'Have another look at the leg.'

Marten had called the controlling manitou of these bug creatures to enter the shaking tent. It told the people it was an iron-clad insect.

A lot of people were sitting around me and they uncovered my leg. They saw a big fat caterpillar, a crawly type thing, coming out. It was already dead, but it was fat with blood it consumed.

By fall I gained enough strength to travel down to Little Grand Rapids, but my knee became stiff from that time on.

26. When Marten Wasn't Around

Thomas Linklater

One spring at Cliff Dweller Lake our family was isolated by break-up. The ice was thin and we couldn't go anywhere. My grandfather, the Marten, was way down at the other end of the lake. There was no way we could get help from him.

This particular spring my father came home and said he had a headache. This was during the time they were practising black magic. We came to believe he was being conjured against; some sort of witchcraft anyways. We knew that he was going to die so we couldn't go anyplace because we were living on the west end of Cliff Dweller's Lake near the little falls. We always lived there in the spring.

My father didn't last very long. He came in complaining he had a headache and by the late night he was gone. I remember earlier in the night he called my brother, he was getting worse. I don't know what he told my brother but he told him about something. My father knew that he wasn't going to make it.

My brother just walked out of there, he didn't say anything. They were very close, travelling together all the time, trapping together. My brother walked out of there. He never came back in again even when my father reached the real sick stage. He knew our father was gone. About three days later, we could make a trip down to my grandfather. He said he knew my father was dying. He said; 'I could do that to a man if I wanted to.'

That's one time I remember, my grandfather wasn't there and we lost the one we loved.

After that my brother went out of his mind. He wasn't himself. He cried most of the time, everyday. He was like that for about six months, until he finally came out of it.

After my father died we were living at Cliff Dweller's Lake, near our winter shack. We could see that someone was out there. Someone set a fire in that thing. Everybody went over there and tried to put the fire out. That fire just flared up. Things continued to happen; weird things. We started seeing things, something would come out, like ghosts. People started to have sickness. Everybody started to have something wrong with them.

Now, if a person doesn't like a man and he wants to put witchcraft on him, he would put something on the trail and when that man passes there, he would pick it up. This is how they do that to each other. If they came home in time to my grandfather, he could perform a kind of miracle for them. This is how he saved people. I know, I used to watch him perform these things.

After this, when my mother took over the family, it was pretty hard for her. There were ten of us kids. My oldest brother sort of took over too, he was nineteen or twenty. But later, my brother went to Red Lake. We moved close to my grandfather after this. We didn't go back to the place where this happened to my dad.

My mother used to say, after my father died, that he would still be looking after us. He's still around and he would know and she would know when he comes in. He would always be checking on us once in awhile. There used to be a sign of a rabbit. That's our sign of our father when he came to visit us. My mother used to say, 'There, your father came and visited us last night.'

We went outside to take a look and see the track. It's here, it's always here.

My mother looked after us even though she was crippled. She was a strong and amazing woman. She brought us up after this. She did the trapping. She taught us how to set the nets. She looked after us well. I can remember after my father died, we were never really in a bad situation or getting hungry. She managed. I don't know how she did it.

Talking about my grandfather's powers, there was a certain time of the year that something would come to tell him to perform the shaking tent. He would tell us to go in the bush and get sixteen different kinds of trees – imagine going out and trying to find sixteen different trees to make his shaking tent because it's time for him to perform again.

This is how we bring back our dead: talk to our dead people with the shaking tent. If you want to talk to somebody, you just ask for it. People were pressured to do that because they wanted to talk to those loved ones that passed away. This is how we used to communicate with our dad – my dad.

From the shaking tent our dad would say that he was still watching over us and stuff like that. A lot of things we would ask him and he would answer us.

It was amazing how my grandfather did it. I mean no man could physically shake that tent. The poles were driven two and a half to three feet in the ground. Sometimes that tent would loosen right up out of the ground. One time I remember, we took a great big rope because that tent was coming off the ground. We couldn't do anything about it. So we tied the rope around the top of it to two big trees near it. The shaking tent made the trees go crazy. Great big trees, not small ones, great big spruce trees. They shook just like little trees.

Before my grandfather, Marten would go in the tent and he would go twice around it, clockwise. Before he reached the point he started from around the tent and before he entered, that thing would start moving. Then he goes in and lays down in there. That tent would really shake then.

There is one person that always comes into the tent. There is always a joker in there. He is the Lynx. He's always there and he calls the dead. He's sort of a messenger there. He tells jokes too – this is the way he is, entertaining. He can be serious at times. He will call the dead people that a person wants to come in there.

Now each person has a different kind of a song. This is how we used to know it was real in the tent. Like my father, he used to sing on the drum. There's a certain song he sang for his own self.

When you go fasting, you have a certain power that nobody knows – and you have your own way of singing it. And people would know if it's the real him that comes into that shaking tent because he would sing that same song. But grandfather didn't know the other people's songs. This is how we used to know my father was there. He would remember my mother and all the things we did. We would ask him all kinds of questions and he would tell us what we wanted to know.

27. Marten Performs for the Hudson's Bay Trader

Thomas Fiddler

There was a Mr. Murray, the store manager at the Hudson's Bay Post in Caribou Lake who was very interested in the shaking tent, although he did not believe it would work. One day when Marten, James Linklater, walked into the store, the

MARTEN AND THE SHAKING TENT, JOHNSON MEEKIS

manager asked him to erect a shaking tent. Marten told him he would undertake this request for five pounds of tobacco.

The shaking tent was built in the clearing in front of the Bay store. The poles that were used were three inches in diameter because the manager insisted they should be that large. Next the tent was lightly covered with birchbark and rawhide and then the top was secured by anchoring thick boat ropes to the ground. It was impossible for any normal human being to shake the structure.

When the Bay manager discovered that the ceremony would be held after sundown as was the custom for all shaking tent rituals, he asked Marten to perform during the day. Marten agreed to this request and he entered the tent in the afternoon. After some time he told the Bay manager to bring five pounds of tobacco into the tent. While the manager was in the tent, he was told to try and shake it but he could not move it the slightest bit. After the manager left the tent the door was closed and Marten was in there for some time. Amazingly, the ropes burst on the top of the tent and it began to shake.

The HBC manager certainly believed in the power of the shaking tent after that ceremony.

The Indians controlled air pressure to operate the shaking tent. Birchbark was placed on the inside of the poles of the tent to prevent air pressure from escaping. A canvas material was used to cover the outsides of the tent also to prevent air pressure from escaping. When the man enters the shaking tent the door is closed to prevent air from going out. However, the door of the tent was left open for a long time before the man entered to allow air to enter – if a man just went in right after the tent was built, it would not work. There must be a certain amount of air in there before it will work.

As I mentioned before – about the manager of the HBC in Caribou Lake – this man left the Caribou Lake post to return to Berens River. During his absence the store was closed and everyone ran out of tobacco because the manager was gone for a long time.

Marten arrived in Caribou Lake and everyone was short of tobacco. Marten had to stay in Caribou Lake until the store opened because he needed supplies. The people were camped on Treaty Point which was about one-half mile across the lake from the trading post. These people asked Marten if he could do something because the people were running out of tobacco. The people had not actually thought of using the shaking tent, but Marten had them build one.

The shaking tent was built in a clearing and a blanket was spread on the ground where the people could sit and watch.

That night when the air pressure had built up inside the shaking tent, the people asked him to go across the lake to obtain some tobacco. He replied that he would do it. The trading post was quite well stocked and it contained lots of tobacco.

When the tent had the amount of air Marten wanted, he told everyone, 'it is ready to go now.'

Twist tobacco was six to eight inches long and about one and one half inches in diameter.

Before the tent starting shaking, Marten asked the people, 'How many pieces do you want?'

'About six pieces,' they replied.

Then the ceremony started and the tent was shaking. But then, the tent slowed down and stopped while Marten was at the store. Then the tent would shake occasionally when he would do something in the store. When he returned, the tent started moving rapidly. The tent stopped, and started shaking again and you could hear someone talking inside the tent. Six sticks of tobacco suddenly landed on the tarp where the people sat but it was impossible to tell where the tobacco came from.

I have not heard whether the HBC has been paid for that tobacco yet!

28. Marten Cures His Brother

Edward Rae

Lots of times I saw Marten trying to heal persons. He had all kinds of medicine that he wrapped up and took to Little Grand Rapids where he sold it. Marten hauled freight with canoes. He was always back and forth between here, Little Grand Rapids and Berens River. The people there were afraid of him. They regarded him as a dangerous man. But he always had medicine for curing. No matter where he went he would heal a person if the payment was sufficient.

One time, Marten accidently shot his brother. The bullet broke his arm, almost right off. Marten fixed his brother's arm right up. Before he healed his brother, he told the people to build a shaking tent. In these days they operate the shaking tent for five days straight. He got the medicine to fix his brother's arm out of the shaking tent. When he was operating the tent, the people would be smoking for him. This tobacco also came out of the shaking tent. The tobacco was in a ball and when it was broken open, it would be a lot. It is almost powder fine, this tobacco, and is mild and sweet to smoke.

Marten, James Linklater, did all kinds of things. He held many dances and feasts. He was a good person.

One time I saw Marten get rough with his wife. He had two wives and he got mad at one and knocked her out for awhile.

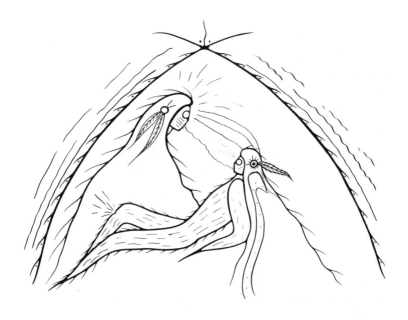

MARTEN CURES HIS BROTHER, JOHNSON MEEKIS

MARTEN CHASES OUT THE BEAVER, JOHNSON MEEKIS

day after this, he went out and walked around. He didn't know
what he was doing. That night he came back to his lodge but he
was out-of-mind. He said he was going to eat all the people.
But his younger brother grabbed him and put him down. His
brother told him he was not going to eat any of the people.
After the fight was over they brought Marten inside the lodge
and he was very sick all night. His son came to him

that night and said: 'I want you to get up – not lie here and die.' The next morning Marten was up and he was okay then but he was a different person again.

Once I was out hunting with Marten and his brother, Henry Linklater. Marten went out of the lodge and did not come back by nightfall. Later that night we heard him singing from across the lake. When he finally returned to the lodge, he threw a rope in the door and told me and Henry to pull the rope. We pulled the rope inside and sure enough, there was a caribou on the end of it.

One time Marten went out hunting and found a bear's den. The entrance was covered up with limbs and twigs. Of course, Marten, got that bear out of there and killed it. Now, a long time ago, they used to say that when a young man killed a bear, he would soon be getting married. When Marten killed this bear he figured he would like another wife but he never did get another wife.

I guess two is enough anyway!

29. Marten, The Old Beaver Trapper

Thomas Fiddler

Marten worked at hauling supplies during the summer and he was hardly ever home. During the winter he was quite a trapper; he was always working at Little Grand Rapids and Berens River, starting in the springtime and he didn't go home until the fall.

During the winter he often went down to Cliff Dwellers Lake to trap by himself. It wasn't very often he went with anybody. He was always hunting and he was interested in hunting up until the time he died. You saw James Linklater last summer, the way he was limping. The winter before this he used to walk down to the hunting lodge to see how it was going. While he was there his grandson told him he knew where there was quite a few beaver and he tried to snare them but he couldn't kill them. His grandson had failed.

Marten went to the place to see if he could kill the beaver.

The place was about one mile away from their camp. He went to the place early in the morning.

Marten made holes in the ice to see where there were openings – where the beavers swam. During this time he was weak from old age. It took him about a day to determine where the opening was and set one snare. When he finished setting the snare he went up on the beaver house and stood on it, trying to flush out the beaver. He flushed the beaver out.

It wasn't very long until his snare pole started waving back and forth. The beaver was killed right there and he hauled it out of the water. But it was too heavy for him to carry, and he didn't want to leave it either. So he started dragging it inch by inch.

When it got late and Marten didn't come back his son told his grandson to go out and look for his grandfather. The Marten was on his way home dragging it inch by inch.

Late in the night they found him on the trail, lying beside his beaver!

Bears and Wolves

PERSONAL EXPERIENCES while hunting and trapping in the boreal north are an extensive part of the repertoire of stories told by Thomas Fiddler and friends. Two of the largest creatures in the forest, the wolf and the bear, are the leading characters in these recollections. It is the consensus of the story tellers that bear is the only man-killer in the dark pine forests. In the previous century hunting bear was an act of manhood. In the old boreal culture, a youth who killed his first bear was said to have proven himself for the responsibility of mating and providing for a family. Thus, honour and prestige are attached to killing this dangerous creature but no such recognition is given to killing the wolf, the little brother of Weesakayjac.

Wolf, in the true stories that follow, is shown in several situations that reveal the character of the little brother of Weesakayjac. Sometimes wolf is frightening because they will attack other creatures who have a closer attachment to human beings. Lowly dogs are given little quarter by wolves even when they are being protected by trappers. In collecting stories for this volume, I was told a story about a wolf. This story was told by a man who frequents the Rushing River. The story is this: At Ogoki Post some of the young people are 'amunis', under a spell, and in the summer one of them drowns in the lake. His parents are full of sorrow, for the loss of a son is a cruel event to endure. In the fall, things are still strange at Ogoki Post. In the winter a wolf begins to walk near the lodges in the night. People see his tracks. Then, people begin to see this wolf in the night. This wolf is unafraid of human beings and, usually he is very very shy. The wolf is around so much, people begin to see him as another presence. The parents of the young man who drowned in the fall see wolf as the presence of their lost son. The parents of the boy are very much concerned that someone might try and shoot the wolf.

They let their feelings about the wolf be known.

In all of these stories there is no evidence of the often maligned wolf attacking a man. Wolf, it seems, is harshly condemned in western mythology because he has the audacity to compete with man the hunter and man the domesticator of many creatures, creatures that wolf has on their agenda of food for survival. *–J.R.S.*

SOLOMON KILLED BY A BEAR, DOUGLAS KAKEKAGUMICK

30. Solomon Wagan Killed by a Bear

Thomas Fiddler

We used to be living down at Mud Lake. There is another lake close by. There is a falls there and a trail near it. One of the men got killed by a bear at this place. His name was Solomon Wagan.

Solomon put up a bear trap there. He caught the bear but it got loose. He only had a little rifle and a little axe with him. The bear dragged the trap quite a distance, but finally Solomon caught up to the bear. When he was getting close to bear, he sensed that he was being followed.

Solomon knew he was getting close to bear and he had his rifle. When he was getting close, he laid his rifle down and took only the axe with him. He saw bear standing in the trees and he approached thinking he was going to kill him with an axe. I suppose Solomon thought he was acting brave and would tell everyone he killed bear with an axe.

The people didn't see it at all but they investigated afterwards and thought about what really happened.

Bear must have got up on its hind legs and when Solomon swung his axe bear must have knocked it away. His rifle was found where he left it.

The people who were living near there were out trapping for a few days and they didn't start to worry until Solomon had been gone about a week. Then they started to think that something must have happened to him. They didn't find him right away. They contacted all the people close-by to let them know that he was gone. They found his boat near the falls and saw his bear trap but they didn't track him, they returned and told the people. They knew he had been killed by the bear. A message was sent down to his family who prepared to come.

When they went to search they found him – this was about two weeks after it happened. Where he was killed, the bear stayed around and they saw him over there. The bear didn't eat the body. The body had decayed in the hot weather so bear didn't eat the body.

31. Francis Meekis Attacked by a Bear

Thomas Fiddler

Francis Meekis was almost killed by a bear too. Francis Meekis was out hunting with Angus Rae. This was when Francis was turning into manhood. Angus was shooting bear. He didn't hit bear well. Finally bear went mad with pain from the wound. Bear took off into the woods and they followed. When they found him, they started shooting again and bear attacked them. When bear charged, Angus took off leaving Francis behind.

Bear attacked Francis. Francis fell to the ground and didn't move. Bear clawed him in the head and in the back. Francis played dead so the bear would leave him alone. Even though Francis was in pain he didn't move. Francis sensed where the bear was after he left him alone. After a while bear went away. When Francis went back to the lake he found Angus sitting in the boat.

32. Thomas Fiddler Calls Up a Wolf Pack

Thomas Fiddler

There was one time I was out hunting moose and a pack of wolves came up to me. This was when I was young, my leg was alright then. I was out on White Island Lake and some wolves came out on the lake. There were about thirty of them. I was walking in the middle of that lake; I had a gun with about fifteen shots for it. The wolves were just running, they weren't coming at me. Then I started howling – ooooooh – like a wolf and the pack stopped for awhile, then they continued running.

I made a wolf sound again. They turned in my direction and came running toward me. I couldn't reach the shore, it was too far away. When they got close I held my rifle. They were close – about two hundred yards and two black ones were closer than the rest. Then, the pack stopped and the two black ones kept coming. I started to yell my head off but I didn't shoot them. They kept on coming closer but I didn't shoot one because I knew the other would eat it. They kept coming slowly toward me. I started waving my arms and they stopped not far off. When they sensed what I was, the two black wolves turned around and started running away. The rest of the pack started running and soon they weren't even in sight.

I was sort of afraid.

33. The Wolves Steal the Beaver

Thomas Fiddler

Another time, in the spring when we were out trapping, myself and my three oldest sons, we caught all kinds of animals and we took them up and stored them in the frozen muskeg so they wouldn't spoil on us. We did this in several places. On this one day, we came back to camp with another load of beaver to store in this muskeg. We had already stored beaver there. We came to the place and there was nothing but a big hole – empty. Immediately, we checked the rest of the caches but they were all the same – nothing. We had lost about thirty beaver.

I told my two sons that just arrived: 'All the beaver are gone.' No one said anything, they just ran up the hill. Losing thirty beaver meant a lot and besides the beaver there were lots of muskrat. We checked again and we didn't find a single one.

Then we started checking for tracks. My two oldest sons went one way and we headed another way. We had not walked very far when we found a beaver foot. When we were looking around we saw a big moss covered mound – like a beaver nest. Our beaver were there, stock piled and covered with moss. We realized who did it: it was wolves. I called my oldest sons and they came running. When they arrived, a wolf started howling. Then wolves started howling from every direction. The wolves had not damaged the beaver except for one foot and they ate another's tail.

I was very surprised the wolves didn't eat the beavers. Now I wonder if wolves will eat beavers at all. So, all the wolves did was take our beavers from one place and put them in another.

WOLF STEALS BEAVER, DOUGLAS KAKEKAGUMICK

Maybe they were going to wait until the maggots set in before they ate them.

During the night, wolves often come near lodges and the people see them but the wolves don't attack. If the wolves were going to attack people, they could have killed lots of children because they are always running around after dark. Around the Sandy Lake area, I have never heard of a man, woman, or child being killed by a wolf.

34. Wolves After Beaver

Abel Fiddler

This happened when I was young. My uncle, Joshua Fiddler, was going trapping and he wanted someone along for company so I went with him. We left in the fall before freeze-up in boats, taking the dog team with us. We went west to the Severn River.

Near Christmas time we decided to come back to Sandy Lake. I wasn't really doing any trapping; I was just there with my uncle. The day before we left, Uncle pulled his traps and snares. He caught one large beaver in a snare and I caught a small one. We sent the dogs and sleigh loaded with our supplies and rifle on ahead by themselves, we often did that; the dogs would go down the river so far then they would stop and wait for us to catch up.

Just after we came up and over Whiteman's Falls we sent the dogs ahead and Uncle and I walked down the river dragging our beaver along behind us. We were somewhere between Whiteman's Falls and Mink Falls on the Severn. A pack of wolves came out of the bush on the north side of the river. The pack leader was bigger than all the rest – you could tell he was leader.

We were walking along the south shore of the river close to the bush. The wolf pack fanned out and spread around us in a semi-circle; my legs were like rubber I was so afraid. I thought it was going to be the end of us. The guns were in the dog sleds further down the river. The wolves were all growling and pack leader was heading straight toward us.

Uncle did not act frightened at all; he took off his pack-sack and pulled out a frying pan and a hatchet – one in each hand. I thought he was going to fight the wolves with them. He walked toward the lead wolf, pounding the bottom of the frying pan with the hatchet. The lead wolf turned around and headed back across the river and the rest of the pack followed him off.

Boy, I was scared that time; my legs were like jelly.

But I have never known of a wolf to attack a man. I think there's lots of food around for them.

The Artists

Sam Ash

Sam Ash was born in Sioux Lookout, Ontario in 1951 and he is a member of the Osnaburgh Band. His mother passed away at birth and Sam, it was soon learned, was a handicapped person for he was deaf and mute. As a child he was reared by foster parents in the hamlet of Umfreville on the Canadian National Railway line east of Sioux Lookout. When he was six years old he was sent to the Ontario School for the Deaf in Belleville, Ontario. He remained in eastern Ontario until 1970 when he graduated from school. He then came north to settle in Thunder Bay and he taught himself to paint. His first one-man show was held at Confederation College in 1973. Much of the content in his early work was based on legends that he read in books but soon his paintings were based on stories that he created. For example, here is Sam's personal legend of the 'Brave Mullets Against Mad Wolf'.

'One morning the mother mullet was leaving its eggs alone so she could look for food to eat. When she returned home she felt shock that one egg was missing from the nest. She heard something wrong and thought there's a Mad Wolf or Hungry Wolf or Evil Wolf at the bush.'

'Later she found that the two eggs would soon break and the little birds would get free of the shell. She must take care of them until they were old enough. After a few weeks she told them about the Mad Wolf. Next morning the two brave young mullets went to find the wolf. While they were gone the mother went to search for something to eat. She didn't know that Mad Wolf was near her. The young birds felt brave and attacked the Wolf. It got scared and was running away. The mother thanked them for saving her life and then they stayed all together.'*

* From: 'Sam Ash: Ojibway Artist,' John A. Warner, Beaver Spring 1977, page 56.

From the start, he received acclaim for his excellent application of paint and boldness of design. His haunting designs are often fluid, appearing as the subject matter of dreams. These designs, which often seem to be floating, have lead one of his patrons to call him the 'Edgar Allan Poe of the native artists.'

Since Sam Ash lives in a soundless world his experiences are mostly visual. One of his forms of entertainment are movies that depict the eternal conflict of the living and dead. Dracula, Frankenstein and other movies of this genre are his favourites. According to his close friend, Noah Sainnawap, Sam is very interested in the 'dark side' of human nature.

Ash's painting is well known to collectors across North America. His work was shown in a collection of Canadian Native Art at the Canada House Gallery in London, England in 1976. He is considered to be first rank among the native artists in Canada.

Levius Fiddler

Levius Fiddler was born at Sioux Lookout, Ontario on February 5th, 1958. He belongs to the Deer Lake Band at Sandy Lake. Levius is the grandson of Thomas Fiddler, the premier story teller in this book. Levius belongs to the Sucker clan, a longtime leading family in the north-western Ontario region. His father, Saul Fiddler, grandfather Thomas, great grandfather Robert, great great grandfather Jack and great great great grandfather Porcupine Standing Sideways have all been headmen of the people in this area. Their English name fiddler was obtained during the 1880s. H.B.C. traders at Island Lake, Manitoba, started to describe these Sucker clan people as 'the Fiddlers' because they started making hand carved fiddles for entertainment.

Levius attended elementary school at Sandy Lake. Here he obtained his first exposure to native art when the late Carl Ray taught a few classes to children at the school. His early inclination, though, was to do landscape painting and occasionally he does this type of work. He did not draw and paint with any regularity while he was in elementary and high school. He sold his first piece of art in 1976. In 1977, Levius graduated from Fisher Park High School in Ottawa. In 1977-78, he attended Confederation College for a year and then returned home to Sandy Lake. He became very interested in painting in 1980 and has worked at this full-time since that date. Levius is basically self-taught but has attended an art course for native artists at Quetico Centre. Some of his painting is done in oils but the majority of his work is in acrylic. He prefers to paint 'human figures rather than animals.'

He is married and presently lives in Thunder Bay.

Gelineau P. Fisher

Gelineau Fisher was born on March 9th, 1951 in the Longlac area of north-western Ontario. He is a member of the Longlac Band. Fisher's inspiration to become an artist began in elementary school where he was exposed to an art class. As a child, Gelineau 'coloured what I saw in every day life. Lots of other kids were more out-coming than I was and for me this was a plus because I was left alone to create.' Fisher tried water colours early but he found them difficult to apply so he switched to pencil, coloured pencils and ink pens to depict his works. 'In my teens,' Gelineau says, 'I took long walks that lasted for hours. I loved every minute of these walks where I sketched on rocks, drew in the sand and wrote my name on everything.'

Fisher, like almost all of the native artists in this book, is self taught. Influences on his art therefore come from many sources. He particularly enjoys abstractionist painting but his own work covers the range from realism to semi-abstract to abstraction.

Becoming a painter, for Fisher, has not been an easy choice. At times he has felt that painting and earning an income from this would only complicate his lifestyle or enlarge personal difficulties. So there have been periods of time when he has not painted at all. Recently he has put these self-doubts behind him and has painted regularly. His approach to painting is 'to use the universe of my mind to create whatever comes out of it.' In this cerebral approach he feels that native peoples 'hurt, pride and happiness play a big part in my work.'

Unlike many of the artists here, Gelineau Fisher is not widely known outside of Geraldton and Thunder Bay, Ontario. Fisher is also a carver and has won prizes for this craft.

He lives in Longlac, Ontario.

Douglas Kakekagumick

Douglas Kakekagumick was born on December 16th, 1958 on the Sandy Lake Reserve. He is a member of the Deer Lake Band. Douglas grew up in a community where native art flourished early. Norval Morrisseau lived in Sandy Lake for a period and other artists from this village include the late Carl Ray, Goyce Kakegamic, Joshim Kakegamic, Roy Kakekagamic, Lloyd Kakapetum, Rocky Fiddler, Johnson Meekis, Saul Mamakeesic and others.

Douglas began sketching when he was in elementary school but it was not until he was a high school student in Thunder Bay that he began to paint seriously. Working in oil and acrylics he began painting legends and stories of his people that had been taught to him by his grandfather, Amos Kakekagumick. Douglas usually pre-sketches his designs before he finally paints. His work is distinguished by clean and sinuous line with exemplary colour composition. Bird and animal life are usually the subject matter in his semi-abstract paintings.

Since 1979, Kakekagumick has painted full time and travelled widely in the country. He has participated in group shows in Vancouver, Winnipeg, Ottawa and Thunder Bay. His work has received recognition from the Ontario Arts Council and some of his paintings are available as prints.

Kakekagumick lives in Winnipeg, Manitoba.

Johnson Meekis

Johnson Meekis was born on April 27th, 1954 in Red Lake, Ontario. He is a member of the Deer Lake Band at Sandy Lake. Johnson completed elementary school at Sandy Lake and went off the reserve to attend high school. While in Grade 10 he married, then spent a year back at Sandy Lake. In 1973, he returned to school, taking an upgrading program at Confederation College. There, he completed a Grade 12 standing then enrolled in Lakehead University where he took the Northern Teachers Education Program. In 1977, he started to teach elementary school at Sandy Lake. After teaching three years he returned to Lakehead University and graduated with both a B.A. in Anthropology and a B.Ed. degree. He returned to teach elementary school in his home village in 1982.

Johnson has been interested in painting since he was in grade four. He saw the paintings of Norval Morrisseau and Carl Ray when he was a youngster but he never saw these artists actually paint. From seeing their results, he began to paint. 'No one ever came to look at my paintings at this time. It was just the joy of creating that inspired me to create drawings and paintings.' In 1974, he had his first art show in the library at Confederation College. His show sold out. He had another show at the Thunder Bay Historical Museum that year, this show also sold out. In 1975 and 1976 Johnson's paintings were part of a Canadian Woodland Indian Art exhibition that toured in Great Britain and Germany. Five of his paintings are part of the permanent collection in the McMichael Canadian Collection in Kleinburg, Ontario.

Being an elementary school teacher has not allowed Meekis to paint full time. In his early years of painting Johnson did pieces that were based on legends. 'Now it's only personal experiences that I paint.' He now has aspirations to create art from stone, wood and metal. Johnson states: 'My one greatest love is the environment that surrounds, feeds, clothes and protects me and my family. This in one aspect of life I don't want to see destroyed.'

Noah Sainnawap

Noah Sainnawap was born on December 25th, 1954 in Pickle Crow, Ontario and he is a member of the Osnaburgh Band. He attended schools at Osnaburgh, the McIntosh Residential School at Kenora and the Shingwauk Residential School at Sault Ste. Marie, Ontario. When he was a child Noah thought he would like to be a priest but his teen years were troubled. 'I dropped out of school in Grade 10 and all I did was get boozed and do drugs and look for easy ways to make money. I never did find an easy way.' It was in a correctional institution where Sainnawap painted his works that sold in 1973. He had listened to a lot of native beliefs from his grandparents. 'My grandparents and my dad were always talking about 'using the mind' and about black magic that was going between different families; evil things travelling in the form of bugs; getting into another person's dreams.' Noah, however, believes only in good spirits like Mother Nature, who he equates as God and this approach keeps him away from difficulty. As an artist he sometimes finds himself as a target of criticism from some native people. This he attributes to the fact that 'artists are a break from tradition and puts me as an artist in a better position to communicate with white people. This makes the artist different from most other native people – artists have become a class by themselves within native peoples. So it's damned hard to be a native artist; hard to get the right breaks. There's lots of competition, there's no steady income. You never know when your next sale is coming. And it's hard to paint while raising a young family.'

Sainnawap is a busy painter, however, and he sells often. His work is spread across Canada, the United States and in Europe. He is, perhaps, one of the most experimental painters in the woodland tradition. His presentations range from complete abstraction to the more traditional semi-abstractions used by most artists. Some of his paintings are pictographic – like rock paintings – while others are appealingly fluid and multi-coloured. Collectors will find his early work signed as Noah, or Noah Brown. All his later work is signed Noah Sainnawap. Sainnawap is multi-talented, he plays the guitar exceptionally well and composes his own songs and music. He also writes poetry. Noah is married and lives in Thunder Bay, Ontario.